The Wealth Algorithm for IT Consultants

The Wealth Algorithm for IT Consultants

The Independent Consultant's Guide to Maximizing Revenues, Tax Efficiency, and Retirement Planning

Eric Chevrette

President, IT360 Financial

First Edition. Published in Canada by BrightFlame Books, Burlington, Ontario. www.BrightFlameBooks.com

ISBN (Paperback): 978-1-988179-71-1
ISBN (Hardback): 978-1-988179-70-4
ISBN (Kindle): 978-1-988179-69-8

Disclaimer

The content of this book is provided for informational purposes only. It is not meant as legal or investment advice and should not be considered a recommendation to purchase or sell any security or products, whether mentioned explicitly or not.

Content contained or made available through this book is not intended to and does not constitute legal advice or financial advice, and no fiduciary relationship is formed. The publisher and the author are providing this book and its contents on an "as is" basis. Your use of the information in this book is at your own risk.

This book is not to be construed as a form of promotion, an offer to sell securities, or a solicitation to purchase securities or products. This book has been produced as a source of general information only. It does not constitute specific advice with respect to your financial situation and should not be construed as financial, legal, accounting, tax or other advice.

The publisher and the author do not make any guarantee or other promise as to any results that may be obtained from using the content of this book. To the maximum extent permitted by law, the publisher and the author disclaim any and all liability in the event any information, commentary, analysis, opinions, advice and/or recommendations contained in this book prove to be inaccurate, incomplete or unreliable, or result in any investment or other losses. Neither the author, IT360 Financial, nor the publisher shall be liable for any loss

Acknowledgements

This book could not have happened without the help and support of many people.

First, I could not have built IT360 Financial into the business it has become had I not been part of a great network of financial advisors through Desjardins and the Desjardins Financial Security Independent Network. Having a great team behind you is incredibly powerful in business, and the Desjardins network has always felt like a vast, supportive extended family.

Second, I had the backing of everyone in my financial centre. Thank you to SFL QMA for supporting me in my adventure. Focusing on a very narrow niche right at the start of my business was a big risk, but they believed in me and let me carve my own path.

Third, IT360 Financial would not be what it is without my team. I have been fortunate to bring together a wonderful group of people. IT360 Financial is built on teamwork, laser focus and innovation, none of which could happen without this exceptional group. Each of them treats the company and, more importantly, our clients as though it were their own business. Every decision they make is with the best interests of the client and the firm in mind, and they are always looking for ways to make things better and more efficient.

Fourth, within the IT360 Financial team, this book would never have happened without one person in particular, Sam Cellini, and his persistence and belief in our mission. He pushed me to put pen to paper and get the story of IT360 Financial out into the world. It took three years, but that persistence and belief paid off. In the end, he mocked up a cover with the company's logo, printed it in colour, wrapped it around a book he picked up off the shelf, and shoved it in front of me so I could visualize what the book would look like. "Eric," he said, "What you and the team have built is incredible. More people need to know it. You need to write a book. This is how we get our mission out there, educate people, and transfer your knowledge to a wider audience!"

Beyond that, he was there throughout the writing process, helping me organize my ideas, contributing client stories and content, and reading and providing feedback on each draft. Sam was also the one who introduced me to Rob Cuesta and the team at BrightFlame Books. Rob helped tremendously with the overall organization and writing of the book, and his team turned everything into the neatly packaged book you are reading now.

Next, I want to thank my family, starting with my parents, who taught me the value of hard work, the personality traits to succeed, and a sense of entrepreneurship, without which I could not have built the business I have. Finally, of course, I thank Nathalie Chabot. She has always been my biggest cheerleader, pushing me to accomplish things I didn't even think were possible. Today, thanks to her, my business brings in more each week than I ever thought I'd make in a year. Beyond that, though, she is also the voice of sanity, telling me when I'm doing something crazy and always willing to tell me the truth—and annoyingly, because she knows the industry and business very well herself, she's invariably right.

Foreword

By Michael Leacy, President, National Association of Canadian Consulting Businesses

I was delighted when Eric asked me to write the foreword for his new book *The Wealth Algorithm: A Complete Financial Guide for Independent Consultants*. In today's dynamic business landscape, the role of independent consultants has never been more vital. You are a driving force behind innovation, growth, and transformation within various industries. Your dedication fuels the success of countless enterprises across Canada.

The Wealth Algorithm is not just another financial guide. It is a tailored roadmap, designed exclusively for independent consultants. It includes decades of Eric's wisdom and insights, as well as best practices, along with contributions from many seasoned professionals who have worked with Eric directly.

The strategies in this invaluable guide will empower you to take control of your finances, maximize your profitability, and secure your financial future. Everything—from managing expenses to optimizing taxes and planning for retirement—is included.

I extend my heartfelt gratitude to Eric Chevrette for his generous work in making *The Wealth Algorithm* a true reflection of the independent consultants' dedication to success. I am honored to present this invaluable resource, and I hope you find it very valuable. Embrace the teachings within this guide and propel your businesses and industry to new heights!

Contents

Introduction

If you're reading this, I assume you're either an independent IT consultant or considering becoming one. I'm also going to assume that you are worried about your finances: how can you make the most of your money, minimize your taxes, maximize your returns, and protect your personal and family wealth for the future? You may be thinking about retirement and wondering whether you'll have enough to see you through your later years. Or you may be much earlier in your professional journey, and you just want to ensure that you can enjoy the benefits of your hard work now but know that there will be enough money for times when you're "between clients."

There's a lot of financial advice out there, and Independent Consultants like you are typically a lot better off than the average Joe (or Jill), which means you probably get approached a lot more than most people by advisors. But how do you know whether the advice you're getting is not just right but *right for you*?

Beware of Broken Paradigms

In Canada, independent business owners like you make up less than 10% of the working population, which means that more than 90% of people are T4 employees. As a result, the financial advice industry is set up overwhelmingly to meet their needs: retail products are set up with employees in mind, and the training which advisors receive focuses heavily on that group. However, you're not a T4 employee:

you're a business owner who owns a corporation, which means you have access to products most people can't buy. More importantly, your corporation is taxed under entirely different rules from other people. That gives you a huge advantage when it comes to planning your finances, as long as you (and your advisor) know how to leverage those different rules and tax laws.

And that's the problem: most advisors you speak to will treat you the same as their retail customers. For them, that corporation you own is just your employer—a 'black box' they don't really understand, and (as far as they're concerned) they don't need to. So, they'll give you good advice—the best they can with the tools and knowledge they have—but it may not be the best advice *for your personal circumstances*. For example, "Max out your RRSP" is good advice *if you're a T4 employee*. However, as you'll discover later in this book, it's not good if you're a business owner.

This is an example of something I call a Broken Paradigm: standard advice and ways of thinking that the finance industry applies because, most of the time, they work. But they break when advisors apply those paradigms to an Independent Consultant like you. The result is a financial environment in which many Independent Consultants miss out on investment opportunities, accept lower returns than they could be making, and pay more tax than they should.

In this book, you'll discover seven of the most common Broken Paradigms that you're likely to encounter when you work with a financial advisor:

1. Fixed-Income bonds to manage risk
2. Salary vs. dividends
3. Income splitting when you shouldn't
4. Assessing risk tolerance

5. Setting RRSP contributions
6. Freezing funds for retirement
7. Leaving estate tax planning to your heirs

The Road to IT360 Financial

Since 2009, I have focused on helping Independent Consultants like you avoid the traps, mistakes, and pitfalls that can easily derail your finances and fixing the Broken Paradigms. And yet, I was never supposed to be a financial advisor. I was born into a family of entrepreneurs in a small town an hour from Montreal, and although I always said I would never work in the family business, fate had other ideas.

When I graduated in 1991, there weren't many jobs available for business graduates. So, I started my professional life working with my father until 1996, when he sold the company to one of Canada's largest paper companies, Cascades. For the next 13 years, I continued growing the business for the new owners as the national sales manager for Canada and USA. All good things come to an end, however, and in 2009 I became my own boss and joined Canada's largest financial services group, Desjardins, as an independent financial advisor. My time working with my father taught me three fundamental lessons that have been invaluable in growing my business:

1. The importance of process.
2. The importance of niching.
3. The value of a "One-Stop Shop."

The Importance of Process

Processes in business are the key to capturing, preserving, and spreading corporate knowledge. When you put systems and processes in place to manage key tasks—whether an admin task like onboarding a new client or a delivery task like requirements gathering—two things happen.

First, as your organization gains knowledge about your clients, what works and what doesn't, and best practices, that knowledge gets preserved and can be shared with everyone who works in the business without having to be relearned time and again.

Second, once you know how to do something well, you can keep doing it well, and as you bring new people into the organization, they can quickly learn how to get the same results. That makes everything you do more efficient and more effective: you know that each time you run the process, you'll get the best results consistently. That is why, in IT360 Financial, we have many processes in place for every aspect of planning our clients' financial affairs to ensure we keep their taxes low and their returns high.

The importance of Niching

A "niche" can mean different things to different people. You probably have a niche: you focus on specific types of work or projects and may even specialize in particular industries (like banks or utility companies, for instance). It's hard to get good at what you do if you're a generalist. The only way to be an expert at many things is to build that expertise at a corporate level: you can't do everything well on your own, but you can surround yourself with a team of really smart people who are each very good at one thing.

When I started my financial advice business in Toronto, I thought, "I'm from Quebec, I work for a French-Canadian insurer, and I'm well connected to the local French-speaking community." Based on that, I decided to focus on serving "French speakers in Toronto." I quickly discovered, however, that some niches are better than others!

It turns out that a niche needs to be about more than common interests or a shared language: the clients you're working with need to have a specific problem (or set of problems). Then you can focus all your energy on getting really good at solving those problems for that group.

Thanks to my links to my target market, I was able to fill my schedule with sales meetings. The problem was those meetings didn't always turn into clients. Why? Because the people I was meeting were all different: they all had different problems that needed different solutions. Today I can laugh about it, but in those early days, it was hard to stay motivated. The big change came when I moved back to Montreal and discovered a group of people who were all dealing with similar issues but had no one who could provide a single solution to the challenges they were facing.

One day, one of my colleagues told me about his brother. He was an independent IT consultant, and he had a bunch of issues no one could help him with. As a business owner, he didn't just need insurance; he needed an accountant, a bookkeeper, a financial planner, a tax advisor, and all sorts of other advice and services. The professionals he had spoken to didn't understand that business owners aren't like "normal" people. However, because I'd grown up in the family business, I saw things very differently. I knew that business owners have different needs and that solutions designed for T4 employees don't work for them. If you treat them like a salaried employee, a business owner will miss out on many of the benefits of being incorporated.

I also realized that if I could fix this consultant's problems, I could do it for others just like him. That is how IT360 Financial was born: a one-stop shop dedicated to helping Independent Consultants like you minimize their taxes and maximize their gains.

The Value of a One-Stop Shop for Independent Consultants

The third key lesson I learned from my dad was the appeal of a one-stop shop: somewhere that provides everything you need without having to shop around for dozens of different suppliers and then try to get them all to work together. Before Cascades bought the family business, they were our competitor. When you're up against a giant like that, you can't win by competing on their terms. You have to be more agile. We were never the biggest player in the market, but we delivered faster and offered more variety. As a result, we were able to put more stuff in each truck that left the warehouse. That was how we were able to thrive in a very competitive environment and hold our own against much larger companies.

I applied the same mentality to building my new financial advice business for Independent Consultants. Just because I was a financial advisor didn't mean the firm could only provide financial advice. Instead, I would assemble a team of highly experienced advisors from other industries and put together the precise package of products and services each of my clients needed. Today, IT360 Financial is a one-stop shop providing everything you need as an Independent Consultant.

As time went on, however, I realized that the real value of working with IT360 Financial wasn't in the range of services we provided. It lies in the depth of expertise we have developed in dealing with Independent Consultants. I'm often called upon to educate professional advisors from many fields—accountants, lawyers, insurance advisors, financial planners, and others—on what Independent Consultants need from them. I'm also a regular speaker at industry conferences in the US and Canada on how to break out of the standard paradigms.

As I said at the start of the Introduction, when you begin looking for advisors, you soon realize that 90% of the professionals you speak to and 90% of the products they offer are geared to the needs of T4 employees, who make up 90% of the market. Very few advisors understand the specific ways in which Independent Consultants differ from T4 employees, and even fewer know how they differ from general businesses: they have different challenges, so they need different solutions.

Very few advisors understand how Independent Consultants differ from T4 employees, and even fewer know how they differ from general businesses.

Why "IT360 Financial"?

Ultimately, you and I aren't very different. As a professional and an Independent Consultant, you follow a code of conduct. Your job isn't to blindly implement a client's instructions regardless of whether you agree with them—especially if you can see that they're putting themselves at risk. You have a responsibility to your client to keep an eye out for anything they might have missed. You watch what's happening in the outside world so they won't get blindsided, and you make them aware of what's going on so they can make a decision based on full knowledge.

When choosing your advisors, the decision shouldn't come down to how smart they are: you can find smart advisors everywhere. Instead, what matters is whether they're paying attention to you—thinking *with* as well as *for* you—and making you aware of new options as they arise so you can make an informed choice based on their advice.

Despite what I said above, it's not as simple as saying, "Everyone else works with T4 employees, but we work with corporations." Our aim is to minimize taxes and maximize financial returns for your whole family at both the corporate and personal levels. So, while we focus on you as a corporation, we take into consideration that you are also an employee, and so (probably) is your spouse. I called my business IT360 Financial because what sets us apart from other firms is that we look at the whole picture, reviewing your finances from every angle. We're not more intelligent than other advisors, but we take a broader view. We look at everything happening in your world and take the initiative to ensure you know what's ahead.

For more than ten years, our philosophy has been to provide everything you need from the start of your entrepreneurial journey to retirement and beyond. We work exclusively with Independent Consultants, assisting them in dealing with their financial needs and challenges, including:

- Tax-efficient investment strategies and insurance products (both corporate and personal) that other advisors do not commonly use
- Incorporation
- Accounting

- Mortgages
- Bookkeeping
- Payroll services

Financial Chiropractic

Many of my clients describe me as their "financial chiropractor." A "regular" chiropractor gets rid of physical pain: sometimes, you use your muscles and joints in the wrong way, and your body starts to complain. If you don't change what you're doing, some of those joints and muscles stop working altogether, and your body tries to compensate, causing more pain and stiffness. Eventually, your body gets used to moving in those inefficient, painful ways, but it's hard to change the bad habits you've picked up and get your body working how it's supposed to. So, a chiropractor uses their skill and experience to release those locked joints and get your body moving how it's meant to.

I do the same with your finances. I make minor adjustments that make your financial pain go away, show you money muscles you never knew existed, and use your money in ways you didn't know it could be used. And bear in mind that sometimes you may not even realize that you have a problem because financial pain, unlike physical pain, is often hidden. But the problem is there whether you know it or not.

Ultimately, my hope is that this book will give you a glimpse of what a pain-free life can be like. After reading it, you'll never think of your finances the same way again.

The Massive Impact of Small Changes

The reason why small changes can make a big difference to your financial fortunes is the power of "compounding," and there's a parable that explains compounding in a straightforward way.

Legend says that a wise man in ancient Babylon presented the great king Hammurabi with his latest invention, a chess set. The king was so delighted that he offered the inventor any reward he wanted. The sage's response seemed modest: he asked for a single grain of rice to be placed in the first square of the board, two on the next, four on the next, and so on, doubling the number of grains each time. King Hammurabi was baffled that the price for this great gift should be so low, but he agreed and ordered the treasurer to make arrangements for the payment.

A week later, the inventor appeared again before the king to complain that he had not received his reward. Angry, Hammurabi ordered his guards to bring the treasurer before him and demanded to know why his order had been disobeyed.

The terrified treasurer threw himself at the king's feet and explained that the reward could not be paid: before he had reached even half the chessboard, the amount of rice required was more than existed in the whole kingdom.

The king's brow furrowed as he thought carefully, and at last, he reached a decision. He had the inventor dragged out into the public square and beheaded.

So, one lesson to take from this is that you shouldn't annoy kings by trying to outwit them. A more useful lesson, however, is what happens when you make a small change and allow the effects to add up over time. This is what drives everything we do at IT360 Financial and allows me to create massive financial changes with minor adjustments—just like a chiropractor.

*When you make a small change in your finances, the effects add up over time. So, make sure any changes you make are **positive**!*

Even a small change adds up over time. For example, a $1 Million investment growing at 8% per annum will be worth $3.17 Million after 15 years. However, just 0.5% extra a year turns that into $3.4 Million—more than $227,500 of additional income. And that 0.5% doesn't come from changing assumptions about future growth: the 0.5% is already there; you just need to "release" it by finding new ways to structure your finances. So, that is what we will be doing together in this book. If you're ready to get started on that process, read on!

Wondering what impact our ideas could have on your wealth? We've created a detailed financial assessment to calculate your net worth at 65 and recommend specific strategies to implement.

Just answer 4 quick questions about your finances.

To get your detailed financial report and recommendations, visit:

https://consultant.financesti360.com/#net-worth-calculator-65yo

Chapter 1

The Taxman Isn't Your Enemy

As an Independent Consultant and business owner, you are locked in a daily struggle when it comes to your finances. Your enemy is cunning and has infiltrated almost every aspect of your personal and professional life.

You're probably thinking this dangerous villain is the government/CRA. But the taxman isn't evil. They're neither good nor bad; they're simply doing a job. They are a fact of life, and the better prepared you are for dealing with them, the less can go wrong. The real enemy is the advice you're getting.

Traditional financial planning is, in many respects, an impossible science based on assumptions and forecasts that require constant tweaking. Taxes, however, are based on rules and facts. And when you understand the rules and nail down the facts, planning becomes much more precise and scientific. That's why, at IT360 Financial, we put a lot of effort into tracking what is happening in tax legislation and the financial markets and ensuring we get the information we need from our clients. It's not infallible—rules and facts change over time—but with this approach, when something does change, the impact can also be predicted precisely (you'll read more about that in future chapters).

Bad advice takes many forms.

- **Incomplete** advice from an advisor who hasn't asked all the right questions (whether because they don't know what questions they need to ask or because their process doesn't allow for those questions).
- **Uninformed** advice from well-meaning friends, family, and colleagues. When someone tells you what to do, ask yourself where their "knowledge" comes from. Even if they're a fellow Independent Consultant, how do you know they're getting the right advice themselves?
- **Out-of-date** advice from someone who has all the right qualifications on paper. The regulatory environment is constantly evolving, but sometimes, the financial advice industry can be slow to catch up.
- **Limited** advice based on an advisor's personal experience and narrow field of expertise: as they say, "When the only tool you have is a hammer, every problem looks like a nail."
- The BIG one: **misdirected or inappropriate** advice. This is the real danger because you're getting advice that would be excellent *for someone else* but is completely wrong *for you*. At best, it's irrelevant and won't do much for you, but at worst, it could cost you and your family a lot of money.

A quick example: When you first incorporated, one of the first things you did was shop for an accountant. Why? Because you understood that you weren't a T4 employee anymore and you had new responsibilities and requirements. You knew you couldn't just go to Staples and buy Tax Return software; you had to get an accountant.

> But did you make the same update in other areas?
>
> If you're like 95% of professionals, you probably kept the same financial advisor you had as a T4 employee. Why? Because there wasn't the same perceived need to get a new advisor. But that doesn't mean it was any less important or less urgent.
>
> And they probably gave you the same advice they did when you were an employee: first, maximize your RRSP, then max out your TFSA, and leave the rest in the corporation to grow.
>
> This is what 95% of the Independent Consultants who come to us have been told. It's good advice (at least you're saving for retirement!), but it's not great. And while the difference between a "good" solution and a "great" solution may look small on paper, over 15 years, it could turn into $500,000 down the drain!

The point is, it's not the world that has changed: the rules for T4 employees are the same as when you were one. It's you that has changed. You're not a T4 employee anymore; you're an Independent Consultant, and you own a corporation. Will the old advice work? Most of the time, yes. But it's not optimized for "You 2.0."

Standard advice aimed at T4 employees will work for you most of the time, but it's not optimized for your situation, and you'll miss many opportunities to maximize your gains and minimize your tax burden.

Now here's the thing. IT360 Financial isn't here to save you; we are here to save you taxes. And it's not about having one brilliant strategy. It's about making many small tweaks, adjustments, and updates, then combining all their effects and compounding them over time, just like grains of rice on your chessboard. Also, this isn't about taking on more risk. It's not about investing in crypto or South African diamond mines. It's about creating structure in your finances.

You'll get more return from paying attention to what's happening in the financial environment and coordinating what you're doing.

As an IT consultant, how many times have you started a project for a client and found that whatever you did to try and patch their systems, things would start to run more slowly each day, systems crashed more often, and eventually, they stopped working altogether? It was inefficient and ineffective. Ultimately what they had wasn't fit for purpose anymore, and the only viable solution was a total overhaul.

When you switch from being a T4 employee to being incorporated, you need the same level of re-engineering. And it's not your fault that you haven't made those changes. You did your best with what you knew and the advice you received. No one told you that you needed to change. The good thing is that, just like a systems upgrade, it's never too late to take things to the next level.

Not all "experts" are equal

Who would you trust to take a scalpel to your head?

a) Someone who once read a Reader's Digest article about brain surgery
b) Your neighbour's cousin's dog walker who had brain surgery last year
c) A brain surgeon
d) A brain surgeon who has performed the exact procedure you need 100 times before on patients just like you and who wrote a book about your condition and how to treat it

The danger when it comes to advisors is that it's one thing to be aware of a strategy on a general level, but being an expert at implementing it is another thing altogether. And knowing how it will interact with and impact other strategies is unique.

It's easy to assume that because your advisor can talk about a strategy, he must be an expert. But how often is he actually implementing it? If his day-to-day business is serving the family market, he's probably not the person you should be listening to.

This is never more obvious than when an Independent Consultant gets in touch with me after a meeting and says something like, "I asked my advisor about this, and he knows all about it. He's going to put it into action right away, so I'm staying with him."

When you take a new idea to your existing advisor, it's easy for them to be a Monday-morning quarterback and, with the benefit of looking at past results and known facts, agree that you could have been doing that for the last ten years. But if the advisor *truly* knew that strategy, why didn't they tell you about it before? You need advisors who are proactive, comfortable dealing with probabilities and unknowns, and future-focused: that's where real value gets added.

Of course, sometimes a Consultant comes back to us and says their advisor told them we're wrong. And I get it: the advisor is simply seeing things through the lens of their experience. Have you ever heard the old saying, "When the only tool you have is a hammer, every problem looks like a nail"? People tend to favour the ideas and solutions they already know, and they don't consider things outside their experience—things that aren't in their toolbox, if you like.

Always remember that advisors are people, too. When you bring them a problem, the first thing they'll do is look in their toolbox—

the strategies they know well and are comfortable discussing with clients. And they won't necessarily consider tools that belong in "someone else's toolbox." Working with something different feels new and—to them, at least—potentially risky, like the first time you get behind the wheel of a racing car if you're only used to driving the family runabout.

It's difficult for an advisor to be an expert in their own field and, at the same time, understand every aspect of the financial environment in depth. What you need is a multi-disciplinary team of highly experienced advisors who are used to thinking beyond the narrow confines of their specialist discipline and working together.

It's challenging to find such experts, and when you do, it's hard to know whether they are actually the right people. Even if you can find them and bring them together, it takes time for them to get to know each other and start thinking across disciplines and collaborating productively. Indeed, I know just how much work it takes to put all that together because I've already assembled that team in IT360 Financial.

A Good Accountant Is Our Greatest Ally

One of the most common meetings we have, not surprisingly, is with an Independent Consultant's existing accountant. Some of them—the more proactive ones—are very comfortable with different financial products, even ones that aren't in their toolbox. They instinctively get what we're doing and see the value we bring to the table. The best will also tell you openly that they don't offer financial products or services. They understand that we're not trying to replace them; we want to partner with them as much as possible. In fact, most of the time, our client's accountant becomes our biggest cheerleader.

A good accountant will look at what we're recommending and immediately grasp at least the principles of what we're doing: the tax subtleties, the financial instruments we're using, and the strategy underpinning everything.

The other kind of accountant knows that what we're talking about is outside their area of expertise, but that only makes them feel threatened. As far as they're concerned, it's not their job to know about investments and insurance, and the strategies in this book are so far outside their model of the world that their knee-jerk reaction is to pooh-pooh them and fill your head with doubt and uncertainty.

> We had a meeting with a potential client in her 60s, Mary. She's a very successful Independent Consultant and has been in the industry for several years. She didn't want to do anything without speaking to her accountant first, so we set up a three-way call with Mary and her accountant. The accountant wasn't a specialist in investments or insurance, but he was curious and open-minded. When we explained what we would do for Mary, the accountant loved it. In fact, he loved it so much that not only did he encourage Mary to sign up with us, he signed up with us himself and started referring other clients to us. That's someone who gets it!

Part of the problem is that accountants tend to think in terms of a two-year window—the last 12 months and the next—not what will happen 20 or 30 years from now. Their focus is on things like dividend strategies, ownership, and corporate structure, and because 90% of their clients run "traditional" businesses, they know what works for store owners, mechanics, manufacturers, etc. They know that the rules are different for Independent Consultants and somehow "harsher," but many of them take an overly cautious approach to protect their client, which means you may end up paying more tax than you need to.

Many accountants know that the rules are different for Independent Consultants, but they take an overly cautious approach, which means you may end up paying more tax than you need to.

So, to minimize your taxes and maximize your gains, you need advisors who think outside the box (specifically, their toolbox!). But don't get me wrong. I'm not saying we're smarter than your advisors. It's just that this is what we do, day in and day out, for thousands of consultants. Because our team has advisors who are experienced in all aspects of financial planning, tax planning, and accounting, we have all the toolboxes open in front of us. And if one person misses something, someone else on the team will catch it. That multidisciplinary team also allows us to watch what's happening everywhere in the business environment and spread what we discover throughout the company. We get these updates through the individual advisors in IT360 Financial and also from our community of Independent Consultants who are constantly sharing and discussing what's going on for them.

I don't want you to think that I'm saying your advisors are deliberately trying to fool you or cheat you, however. They have good intentions and give you the best advice they can with the information you provide. But they may not know everything they need to ask (because they're used to working with employees, not a corporation) or what to do with the answers you give them (because it's not what a T4 client would tell them).

Don't try this at home, kids!

You're probably thinking you could do this all yourself—after all, you're a smart guy. You could find a tax advisor, an accountant, an insurance broker, and an investment advisor who work exclusively with independent professionals, then try to piece together all the information they give you.

Think of it like baking a cake with lots of people giving you ideas for ingredients. Someone tells you to put in some blueberries; another wants orange. Someone else wants peanut butter, and maybe you like lemon.

Those are all delicious ingredients in their own right, and there are many wonderful cakes that can be made with them. So, you could throw them all into the mix and see how the cake turns out. Or you could work with someone who can go through that list of possible ingredients and tell you which combinations work well, which won't taste nice together, which will make you bloated, and which will stop the cake from even rising.

That's what we do for your finances: we tell you how all the ingredients of an investment strategy combine, what works well together, and how each element affects the others. It's what we call your "Corporate Investment Policy," and it sets IT360 Financial apart from other advisors you may have worked with. So, let's see how it works.

Chapter 2

Corporate Investment Policy

The best way to minimize taxation is to allow your money to accumulate in your corporation and only take out what you need to cover your living expenses. Everything else stays inside the company, so you can take advantage of the investment opportunities and tax breaks that corporations enjoy.

Your Corporate Investment Policy governs how you'll build your financial pot in every phase of your professional life, from when you start working with us until your estate is settled. It sets out how much you'll invest and when, the asset classes you'll use, the ratio between them, the order in which you'll make deposits and withdrawals, and every other aspect of managing your investments and building a fully diversified portfolio.

Your Greatest Business Asset (It's Not What You Think It Is)

Before I set out how a Corporate Investment Policy works, I want to address something that most Independent Consultants don't think about enough. Because there is one thing that everything else in your business depends on: your ability to earn income. If you can't make money, there is no wealth inside the corporation to grow, and you don't have a business. That is why one of the first things I check with a new client is that they have Disability Cover in place. And if they don't, we have a deal with a major financial institution to provide coverage at a substantial discount below the typical market rate. Unlike other insurances I discuss with my clients, Disability Cover is not about tax efficiency or investment growth. This is the one time we use insurance purely for protection, and it's crucial, which is why we discuss it before anything else.

Buying Disability Cover is one case where you should pay for the policy personally rather than through the company. When you do that, any payouts you receive are tax-free, which means you need less insurance. And as an additional benefit, Disability Cover is one of the things CRA may consider when evaluating your tax status as an Independent Consultant[1].

Now that we've addressed why it's essential to protest your ability to earn money, let's look at your Corporate Investment Policy (and here, I'm using the word "policy" to refer to the rules and standards you set yourself to govern how you invest your money).

We structure your Corporate Investment Policy around three pillars.

1. Protecting and increasing your net worth.
2. Establishing your own pension plan.
3. Structuring a tax-efficient investment portfolio.

---

[1] To ensure the currency and credibility of our information sources, and to obtain documentation supporting our assertions, please contact us at marketing@financesti360.com to access our references.

Protecting and Increasing Your Net Worth

The first pillar of your Corporate Investment Policy generates tax-efficient investment growth while cushioning you from shocks in the financial markets. The aim is to eliminate the need for low-return fixed-income investments in your portfolio. Instead, we focus on products that are low risk, with a higher return but taxed at a lower rate. And since the aim is to protect wealth, you probably won't be surprised when I tell you that we use insurance products for this. What might be more surprising is that we are using insurance with the aim of *increasing* your wealth.

Usually, when I discuss insurance with a potential client, their eyes glaze over. It's not an exciting topic for most people. And who can blame them? When people think about insurance, they think of protection, not financial returns.

One of the most helpful shifts you can make in your financial thinking is your attitude toward insurance and how it's used. If you're accustomed to thinking of it in terms of protection, like most people, you probably pay a few thousand dollars a year in premiums on different policies. And for most people, that's all they need. But you're not like most people: you're an Independent Consultant and a business owner. So, you need to ask yourself, "How ***else*** can I use insurance?"

Insurance Is an Investment, Not an Expense

If I suggested you put $20,000, $30,000, or even $50,000 into your policy, you'd probably tell me I was crazy. That's because you're still thinking of insurance as protection, not as an investment to help you to reach your financial goals more quickly. After all, would you have a problem if I suggested you put the same amount into fixed-income investments or a pension?

When it comes to insurance, most people just focus on two things:

1. What's the absolute minimum level of cover they need?
2. How can they reduce their premiums?

That's the mindset of a T4 employee. However, as a business owner, you need to understand that there are many ways to use insurance in a corporation to your advantage. In fact, in the corporate environment, insurance products are taxed very favourably. So, the right insurance products can be one of the best ways to both protect you and your family and, at the same time, optimize your financial returns while minimizing the tax you pay on your gains.

Many financial advisors overlook this use of insurance; they only see it as a way of protecting you against risk. At IT360 Financial, we ensure our clients carry enough insurance to deal with the unexpected. However, we also look for opportunities to use insurance as a tax-advantaged investment. When you use it that way, as I said above, it behaves a lot like a fixed-income bond but with a much better and more predictable rate of return.

Of course, some people don't like making long-term commitments. But you wouldn't question committing to pay into an RRSP. And if you were in a company pension plan, you wouldn't have a choice: your employer would simply tell you, "We're taking 8% of your salary and putting it into your pension."

The key is not to think of the payments you make into your policy as a premium (which is a cost). Instead, think of it as a *contribution* (to an investment), just like payments into a pension.

Broken Paradigm #1: Fixed-Income Bonds to Manage Risk

Imagine a consultant—we'll call him Jim—who has a $250,000 portfolio. If he's like most people, that money will be invested in what we refer to as a "growth" portfolio: 30% fixed-income investments (typically bonds) and 70% stocks. The problem with bonds, however, is that while they provide predictability, returns are very low and taxed at 50%. So, Jim makes very little money on those investments, and the government takes half of whatever gain he does make. To get out of that broken paradigm, Jim needs something that looks and acts like a fixed-income investment but isn't one.

The role of these fixed-income investments in Jim's portfolio is risk mitigation. So, we need products with low financial risk. By using insurance instead of bonds, we can provide Jim with a product that not only provides lower risk but also gives a higher rate of return, protects him from unforeseen events, and allows him to withdraw retained earnings from the corporation tax-efficiently.

Of course, if you're used to thinking of insurance as an expense, you're probably wondering how it creates a return. It's all down to the tax treatment of different products, and those differences can give you 3x to 5x more revenue than a regular fixed-income investment. So, in IT360 Financial, we consider insurance a key component of financial planning for a corporation, and we use it for tax minimization and deferment, not just protection.

In fact, we use two specific products. The first is our Estate Retirement Plan, a very clever life insurance policy designed for business owners, and the second is an equally clever critical illness policy which we call the Executive Health Plan.

The Estate Retirement Plan

As I said earlier, the Estate Retirement Plan (ERP) is really a very carefully designed life insurance policy taken out not by you but by the corporation. The ERP is a perfect example of the way that IT360 Financial is always thinking about the future and the impact your financial arrangements today will have in retirement and when you die.

There are three major benefits to setting up an ERP how we do.

1. Of course, it's a life insurance policy, so it's there to protect your family if you should die prematurely.
2. The ERP is there to generate a steady income for you tax-efficiently when you retire (in what we call the Withdrawal Phase, which you'll read about later).
3. When you do die, it ensures that there will be money available to pay the taxes on any inter-generational transfer of wealth (something we'll return to when we discuss the Succession Phase).

So, if you die early, your family is taken care of. But if you don't, you haven't thrown away the money you paid into the ERP: you can take it out as a regular income when you retire. And the way we designed the ERP, there will still be enough left when you finally go to the great golf course (or yacht club or whatever) in the sky to make sure your family can pay any tax due on the transfer of your estate. So, it gives a great return on investment for something most financial advisors wouldn't consider an investment!

The ERP provides protection for your family if you die early and a steady tax-efficient income if you don't.

You'll learn more about the ERP later in the book. For now, let's look at the other product in this pillar, your Executive Health Plan.

The Executive Health Plan

The second strategy is the Executive Health Plan (EHP): you pay an annual premium for a fixed number of years, and if you are diagnosed with a critical illness in that time, the policy pays a tax-free lump sum to the corporation.

> One of our clients was 38 when she was diagnosed with ovarian cancer. Fortunately, she had the Executive Health Plan, which allowed her to stop working. She received $500,000 immediately into her corporation and a personal monthly payment from her disability coverage—all tax-free.

That's the protection aspect of the product, but as I said, it's hard to get excited about protection. So, why am I so passionate about this strategy? Because of how the premiums are taxed and what happens if you *don't* claim.

Imagine your corporation takes out a 15-year plan which will pay $1 Million if you fall ill, with an annual contribution of $30,000—that's a total of $450,000 invested over the term of the plan. Each year, however, only part of that contribution is treated as a taxable benefit and added to your personal taxable income. The rest incurs no additional tax liability. And if you stay healthy, then at the end of the 15 years, the full $450,000 will be paid out to you personally with no additional tax to pay.

If, instead, you decided to simply withdraw $30,000 from the corporation each year as personal income, it would all be taxable at your marginal tax rate. So, the question is, do you want to pay tax on the whole $450,000? Or would you prefer a more tax-efficient strategy where the corporation pays a third party to protect you in the event of a critical illness, and only part of the premium is treated as a taxable benefit?

Because of how the product we use in your EHP is structured, that's precisely what it does for you. Your Executive Health Plan is taken out for a specific length of time. If you don't make a claim, then at the end of that time, all the money the corporation has paid into the policy comes back to you *personally* with no further tax implications. That's why in the example above, at the end of the 15 years, the insurer would pay you (not your corporation) $450,000, and there's no additional tax to pay.

Now, you can also think of the tax savings on your premiums as profit, at which point the policy starts to look like a fixed-income investment. But if you had simply kept that money inside the corporation and invested it, you would pay tax on the gains, and when you took the money out of the corporation, you'd pay tax on that, too.

Of course, there is a challenge with this strategy. The other strategies in this book are available to everyone as long as they meet the relevant requirements. You sign the papers, and everything is in place. However, insurance is linked to your health. So, if you have any preexisting health issues, the exact terms you get will depend on the offer an insurer is willing to make.

That's why you need the right advisor who can look at the whole picture and decide exactly what strategies to put in place based on your personal situation.

Establishing Your Own Pension Plan

The second pillar of your Corporate Investment Policy is establishing your own pension plan. Most small business owners don't know that in Canada, even the smallest company can set up an employee pension plan just like major corporations, and the company's contributions are deductible expenses.

In Canada, even the smallest company can set up an employee pension plan just like major corporations, and the company's contributions are deductible expenses.

So, why doesn't every small business owner create a company pension plan? Because setting one up from scratch and managing it is complicated and expensive. You need to hire lawyers, actuaries, and fund managers. That's why IT360 Financial partnered, instead, with one of the largest pension fund providers in Canada to create a product called the Executive Pension Plan (E-PP) which makes the process as easy and pain-free as possible.

Instead of you having to hire a team to run your plan, we set it up, look after it, and work with your accountant so that everything is reported to CRA correctly (so you can enjoy the tax benefits).

E-PP vs. RRSP

T4 employees can put money into an RRSP, but that has several disadvantages and limitations compared to an E-PP. First, you can never put more than 18% of your salary into an RRSP. Second, fund managers charge fees for administering the plan—typically up to 2.25%—and those fees are subject to sales tax and aren't a deductible expense.

For a corporate pension plan (including an E-PP), the situation is very different. Let's start with the administration fees: for a corporation, those fees aren't subject to sales tax, and they're a deductible expense. So, you're saving money compared to a salaried employee with an RRSP. More importantly, however, you can make much higher contributions if you want to. Instead of being capped at 18%, your contribution limit increases with your age, up to 30% of salary. So, your pension fund can accumulate much faster than an RRSP.

And if you've been in business for a while, that's no reason you should miss out: you can "buy back" years of service from the date of incorporation by making payments for the years you "missed." So, if you've amassed a lot of cash in the business and you're wondering how to use it tax-efficiently, you might have a buyback opportunity that allows you to invest a six-figure lump sum into your E-PP to minimize tax.

If you have surplus cash in your business, you may have an opportunity to invest it tax-efficiently by "buying back" the years from when you incorporated.

How it Works

On the surface, an E-PP looks and acts just like the private pension funds major corporations operate for their employees. There is a pot of money ringfenced in your name, to which your corporation contributes and from which your benefits will be paid when you retire. Behind the scenes, however, it's managed collectively with all our other Independent Consultant clients across Canada who have an E-PP. That means the pension provider treats us like a major corporation with thousands of members in our pension plan and gives us rebates and lower fees.

If you have an existing RRSP, we can also transfer it into the E-PP so you can enjoy deductible fees on your whole pension pot (so it grows even faster). And, if you have historic unused RRSP contribution room, we can use it in your E-PP by making an Additional Voluntary Contribution (AVC)—a discretionary payment made by the company that allows you to use excess RRSP room tax-free. Once the E-PP is up and running, it automatically uses your RRSP headroom each year, so you don't need to worry about it.

And the kicker is the portfolio behind that plan. Earlier, I described the typical growth portfolio: 30% fixed-income and 70% stocks. Most RRSP portfolios and retail pension plans contain a broadly similar mix of investments. Fixed-income investments will be a combination of Canadian government bonds, corporate bonds, and maybe some foreign government bonds. On the stock side, they'll similarly have a mix of Canadian and US stocks and perhaps some investments in emerging markets.

Over the last 15 to 20 years, a good RRSP fund manager was lucky to achieve a 7% average annual return with that sort of portfolio. In the same period, managers in the biggest private pension funds—Ontario Teachers, or any major corporation with an employee pension plan, for example—typically made returns closer to 9%. Now, an extra 2% might seem small, but remember compounding. If you started with a lump sum investment of $100,000, then after 15 years of growing at 7%, your fund would be worth just under $276,000. At 9% per year, however, that same investment would be worth just over $364,000 ($88,000 more) thanks to the power of compounding.

Why are the managers of these big pension funds able to get higher returns? It's not that they're more intelligent than RRSP managers. It's just that they have access to investments that RRSPs don't. If you were to examine the portfolios of those big private pension plans, you would find that typically 35% to 45% of the fund is invested in what are known as "non-traditional investments": major infrastructure projects, private lending, commercial property, agricultural land, etc.

If you tried to set up a private pension plan yourself, you wouldn't have access to those high-return non-traditional investments either. You'd be stuck with the same kind of portfolio as the RRSP managers. The E-PP, however, opens the door to those investments. But even if we ignore non-traditional investments, if we compare two people with the same taxable earnings, one contributing the maximum possible into an RRSP throughout their working life and the other putting the maximum possible into an E-PP, the E-PP holder still comes out ahead because of the favourable tax treatment their plan enjoys.

> Imagine two identical twins, Jim and Mike. They went to the same university, and after graduating, they both became Independent Consultants. They both started preparing for retirement at the same time, but Jim set up an RRSP and maximized it because he didn't know any better, while Mike put his money into an E-PP.
>
> Now, let's assume Jim and Mike are identical in every other respect: they have the same level of risk tolerance, their costs of living are similar, and their rate of return on investments is identical.
>
> By the time they reach retirement age, Mike's E-PP portfolio will be worth at least double the value of Jim's RRSP portfolio.
>
> And it has nothing to do with financial performance: it's all down to the tax advantages enjoyed in an E-PP over an RRSP.

It's not unusual for an E-PP to end up being worth twice as much as an RRSP in those circumstances. Why? Because the higher contribution ceiling in an E-PP allows you to put more money into the pot (so it grows faster), and you're saving money in fees and taxes. For every dollar you put into your E-PP, the tax deductions on the contributions alone equate to a 12% return on investment in Ontario and 20.5% in Quebec (other provinces will vary, but it will always equate to a greater rate of return, no matter where you live). And as the pot grows, tax on that growth is deferred until you take the money out, just like an RRSP.

Once you factor in the higher returns from non-traditional investments, it's not unusual for the E-PP fund to be three times what the RRSP fund would be: so, if you were going to retire with an RRSP fund of $500,000, you could end up with $1,500,000 in an E-PP to fund your retirement instead. That's why, whenever a client asks me, "Eric, should I be paying into an E-PP?" the answer is Yes!

With an E-PP, you will have access to an investment vehicle that:

1. has an increasing contribution limit as you age,
2. gets beneficial tax treatment,
3. gives you access to higher-return investments,
4. with fees that are tax deductible and aren't subject to sales tax.

Why wouldn't you take advantage of that?

At this point, you're probably thinking, "But Eric, you told me you don't use any products that aren't available to other advisors. Now you're saying there's a secret product called an E-PP that no one else can sell me!" Here's the thing. You won't have heard of an E-PP, but you may have heard of an Individual Pension Plan (IPP). Many accountants and financial advisors hate IPPs because they are complex to set up and expensive to run—you need a trust, a money manager, and an actuary. Before I became a financial advisor, my dad had an

IPP, so I've seen firsthand just how messy they are to set up and run. That's why I knew that I needed something simpler for my clients.

On the face of it, an E-PP looks very much like an IPP: they're both ways to create your own pension plan. Furthermore, IPP management fees are deductible like an E-PP (and unlike an RRSP). However, under the surface, the two are *very* different. The E-PP brings all the running of the plan under one roof, so instead of managing everything yourself (or getting your accountant to do it), it is administered on your behalf by one of Canada's largest pension groups. So, you don't need an actuary, an in-house fund manager, or a trust. Of course, there is still some work for your accountant to do, but because we've done this so often, we've created a set of "paint-by-numbers" instructions for them that eliminates the admin hassles that may have put them off in the past, and we have a dedicated in-house team that only works on E-PP for our clients.

Should you put your money in an RRSP or an E-PP?

Do you want to maximize your retirement plan? Is an RRSP really your best option? We've created an online calculator to compare your potential net worth at age 65 after investing in an RRSP vs. an E-PP. To discover how much better off you could be, answer a few simple questions at

https://consultant.financesti360.com/#compare-rrsp-vs-epp

The E-PP also addresses many of the weaknesses of an IPP from the entrepreneur's point of view. For example, a major downside of IPPs is that the best time to set one up is at age 45-55; if you're outside that range, there's not much you can do. You can set up an E-PP at any age, however, and as I said above, backdate it to when you started your business.

Structuring a Tax-Efficient Investment Portfolio

The third pillar of your Corporate Investment Policy is to put your investments into a carefully designed tax-efficient structure we call a Corporate Portfolio. This represents money not invested long-term in your pension plan or insurance. So, it's available for whatever projects come up (buying a holiday home, taking the cruise of a lifetime, buying a boat, or whatever), for life events like paying for your kids to go to college, and for emergencies. However, just because you don't know when you'll need that money, that doesn't mean we leave it in a bank account. Instead, it's invested so that it can work for you and grow.

I've already said that a standard "growth" portfolio comprises 30% fixed-income investments and 70% stocks. However, when it comes to investing your money, we're not going to put 30% of it into bonds and pay 50% tax on what little money you make from them. The key is to treat all the money in your corporation as one huge portfolio. If you've invested in the first two pillars, then you already have money in solutions that act like fixed-income investments: insurance in the first pillar and your E-PP in the second. These help to manage volatility in your overall portfolio, which means that we can be more growth-focused with our investment approach in the Corporate Portfolio while maintaining the overall balance of risk and return.

In your Corporate Portfolio, we invest mainly in stocks, which will generate capital gains. Unlike other income, only 50% of a capital gain is taxed at a standard rate of 50%. So, already, we're paying less tax compared to investing in bonds.

The problem for most corporate investors is that if you hold stock directly—in what's called an Open Portfolio—not all gains get that beneficial treatment. If you directly own stock in a foreign company, say Microsoft or Alibaba, the gains aren't just taxed at 50% of 50%. In fact, you can end up paying as much as 68% tax on them.

To get around that, we create what is known as a Corporate Class Portfolio. Instead of investing directly in non-Canadian stocks, we put them into a Canadian investment company inside your own corporation. That way, you get to enjoy the benefits of those foreign investments, but from a tax standpoint, *your* money is invested in a Canadian company, so you qualify for the lower capital gains tax regime. This structure also allows you to benefit from deferred Canadian capital gains even if you're investing in emerging markets or other foreign companies. In other words, you don't have to pay taxes on your gains until you need the money.

Here's what that looks like. Imagine you've invested $50,000 each year for three years, and over that time, the value of your portfolio increased to $200,000—a $50,000 gain. While that's accumulating, you don't have to pay any tax, personally or in the corporation. Now, let's say something comes up, and you need to take it all out—maybe you want to buy a cottage. To do that, the investments in the portfolio will have to be sold, and when you do that, the gains "crystallize," and the tax stops being deferred.

The corporation pays no tax on the first $150,000 of the proceeds because that was the original capital investment. The rest of the money—$50,000—is the capital gain, and as I said above, the corporation will pay 50% tax on 50% of it. So, CRA gets $12,500, leaving $187,500 for withdrawal to your personal account. To make that withdrawal, first, you can pay yourself half of the gain ($25,000) tax-free. That leaves $162,500, which you take as a dividend on which you pay personal income tax at your marginal rate.

Do You Have Everything in Place?

If what you've just read is making your head spin, here's a quick check you can do for yourself. Are any of the following true?

- ☐ You make the maximum contributions to an RRSP each year.
- ☐ You don't have an E-PP in place.
- ☐ You pay yourself dividends instead of salary.
- ☐ You pay yourself more than you need each year and put whatever is left into a TFSA.
- ☐ You regularly have more than $20,000 in your personal bank account at the end of the year.
- ☐ You're not using insurance strategically inside the corporation.

If you answered "yes" to any of those questions, you might be reducing your overall wealth and paying more tax than you need.

How Much Should You Put into Each Pillar?

So, we've seen that your corporate investment policy has three pillars:

1. Protecting and increasing your personal wealth with an Estate Retirement Plan and Executive Health Plan.
2. Preparing for retirement with an Executive Pension Plan.
3. Structuring your investments tax-efficiently in a Corporate Portfolio.

That leaves a fundamental question: how much money should you put into each pillar? For that, we need a system that will analyze every financial decision you face and tell you the implications for your tax now, the tax you will pay in the future, and the value of your overall wealth portfolio. So, it's time to introduce something we like to call simply "The Tool."

But first, let's look at these ideas in practice with one of our clients.

Case Study 1

In the Driver's Seat: Matt Gervais

For Matt Gervais, control is a driving force. He became a consultant in order to take control of his work, and through working with IT360 Financial, he enjoys being in control of his financial future.

I'm an Independent Consultant with my own consulting company. There's only one employee: me. I work primarily with the Canadian Federal Government, helping them implement cloud services, specifically using Microsoft tools—Office 365, Dynamics 365, and MS Power Platform—to improve business productivity and serve Canadians in the most effective way possible.

I started my IT Solutions career as an employee for Bell Canada, then joined the Solutions and Services Division of Microsoft Canada. I could see that the Federal Government was moving towards public cloud services and that Microsoft was uniquely positioned to take the lion's share of that business. But I soon realized there was a significant gap between where the customer was in their cloud journey and what the technology could provide them. There was a fundamental disconnect between what the company had hired me to do and what the government was ready for, and eventually, I was laid off.

That was the event that catalyzed me to become an Independent Consultant. Of course, there are benefits to being an employee of a major corporation like Microsoft: you get exposure to big clients, and you have the company's brand behind you when you speak to them. But at the end of the day, you're just a number; your employer has all the power and control in the relationship, and one day you get a tap on the shoulder, and someone from HR says, "Okay, thank you very much. Here's your severance package. Have a good day."

So, becoming an Independent Consultant was very much about control. I can decide what I do, how much I work, when, and even where and for whom. My success is totally down to me. Even though I'm a "hired gun," if I can show solid knowledge, understanding, and leadership, the client will listen, and we can work together productively. This gives me control of my destiny.

The key word for the client is *independent*. They have direct access to their vendor—whether that's Microsoft, a Big Four consulting firm, or whoever—but they know that the company's employees are ultimately loyal to their employer, not the customer. As an Independent Consultant, the client sees me much more as "one of their own" (after all, they're signing my pay cheque). So, they'll say things, ask questions, and have conversations with me that they couldn't have with one of the vendor's employees. They may even ask for my opinion about the vendor and what they're advising!

And that brings me to one of the biggest changes I noticed in moving from being a full-time employee on the vendor side to being an Independent Consultant. As an employee, my loyalty and focus were divided. Of course, I had to take care of the customer and keep providing value to them as their representative. But at the same time,

I had to keep my employer happy, look after their interests, and ensure that I was providing value to them.

That can be more stressful than you'd think. In fact, my wife has commented that I'm much less stressed these days, which might seem surprising to anyone who still equates job security with permanent employment and a regular pay cheque. When I became independent, one of the first things that hit me was the relief that I could stop worrying about Big Brother. Instead, I can be laser-focused on my client and what they need.

Of course, the most significant benefit of being an Independent Consultant—or at least the one everyone thinks about—is the money. An employee's pay is determined by corporate salary bands, budgets, the hierarchy, tenure with the company and all the other stuff that goes with being part of the corporate world. As an Independent Consultant, however, my rate is based on market demand. And fortunately, demand for my services is going up and up, and so are my rates.

Since 2016, my rates have increased consistently by 20-30% each year. And as my experience grows from one project to the next, so does my justification for those rates. Compare that to what would have happened as an employee: unless I got a promotion or changed employer, I might have gotten a few percent pay rise, or more likely, I'd still be on the same salary as I was three years ago.

Many employers asked their staff to take a pay cut during the Pandemic. For me, however, the Pandemic actually boosted my revenue significantly as the need to support work-from-home and online business collaboration increased demand for cloud-based services even faster.

Over the last couple of years, several companies have asked me to join them as an employee. While they're great companies and nice people to work with, I keep coming back to my big driver, which is control: I don't see how I could be a staffer and still enjoy the flexibility I now have and the ability to set my own parameters for how and when I work. So, I'd be losing control and taking a pay cut!

Some people think they're still better off on a salary, even if it's lower, because of the benefits: pension, paid leave, medical insurance, etc. As an Independent Consultant, I can choose where I put my money and what benefits I want to buy for myself, and I don't have to pay for the overheads that a major corporation has to carry. I'm not paying for someone else to sit in a big office or drive an expensive company car.

Everything I earn—everything that my output is worth—comes directly to me, and I decide how to spend it. Of course, the flip side is that I'm responsible for my finances. But I also have much more control over how my affairs are managed.

In the early days, I was contracting as a business analyst, and I only commanded a certain level of fees—not much more than I'd been earning at Microsoft. Only later in my contracting career did I see a significant rate increase. So, initially, I didn't look for independent financial advice. Instead, like most new consultants, I set up a spreadsheet to track money coming in and how much I was paying myself. My father-in-law is a tax preparer, so he advised me on what percentage to keep back for CPP and Income tax and how to send remittances to CRA.

Because I wanted to take home as much as possible, I paid myself a minimal salary and maximum dividend and sorted out my income taxes at the end of the year. Of course, it meant I had to make sure there was enough money left in the business at the end of the year, but business was good, so I didn't see it as a problem.

As time went by, however, things got more complicated. I was dealing with more contracts, and with more revenue came higher tax rates. I also wasn't doing anything to plan for retirement.

Fortunately, I was introduced to IT360 Financial through one of the staffing firms I worked with, Cofomo. That's how I discovered that I had been building up a tax headache by paying myself mainly in dividends and getting the corporation to pay my taxes. After all, I thought, it's all my money, so what difference does it make whether I pay the bill or the company does?

As it turns out, it makes a big difference!

And, as my revenue and the tax bills increased, the problem just compounded year after year.

Thanks to IT360 Financial, I got the advice I needed to resolve the problem, and we've changed how I pay myself so it won't happen again. I take more salary than dividends, and I have a payroll company that makes all the CRA/CPP deductions and remits them throughout the year, which keeps me on track. Then I work with the team at IT360 Financial to deal with the revenue in the company and plan for retirement in the most tax-efficient manner.

And speaking about retirement (though it's still many years in the future), what I'm most looking forward to is the opportunity to work less. It's all back to my big driving principle of control. As I get closer to retirement, I'll be able to slow down without worrying about what an employer thinks of me or whether enough money is coming in to pay the bills, maintain my lifestyle, and support my family financially. The way things are set up with IT360 Financial, I'm taking advantage of this time where I'm working hard and probably making the most I'll make in my consulting career by maximizing my investments. As I get closer to retirement age and work less, I'll draw on those investments to bring my income up to levels I've grown accustomed to. But thanks to IT360 Financial, I'll be doing it tax-efficiently.

When I started working with IT360 Financial, they made a significant up-front investment of time in me. Instead of jumping straight in with a shopping list of products they wanted to sell me, they shared their knowledge and experience and helped me understand my financial situation very deeply. It was a lot of free consulting, which provided great value and allowed me to get to know them before I had to commit to anything. That was very different from other financial firms I'd spoken to.

I love working with Sam, Eric, and the team, and I've told several colleagues about them. I have a community of fellow cloud architects that I'm very close to. Like me, they're great technically, but they're not strong on finance and pensions. So, I introduced them to IT360 Financial because I knew they could use the help!

Chapter 3

Modelling Your Financial Future: "The Tool"

Clients are often surprised that we don't have a pile of brochures in IT360 Financial for everything we do. The reason we don't is simple. I prefer to illustrate using your personal situation rather than make you read a bunch of generalizations you will have to piece together. So, when we sit down with an Independent Consultant, we put everything through a proprietary financial planning model we affectionately call The Tool, developed over the last 15 years by our resident genius, Dany Provost.

Dany is among the best-known figures in the financial services industry: regularly featured on TV, radio, and in the press, author of two books, including the best-selling *Arrêtez De Planifier Votre Retraite, Planifiez Votre Plaisir* ("Stop Planning Your Retirement; Plan Your Fun"), and frequently consulted by other financial experts on many areas of taxation, individual insurance, financial planning and group insurance. After evaluating many of the planning models in use in the financial advice industry, Dany realized that none of them were optimized for business owners. So, he created his own—The Tool—which he constantly tweaks and updates to stay in line with changes in tax laws, financial regulations, and whatever is happening in the financial markets. He is always thinking several steps ahead, and by the time a new tax law comes out, he's already adjusted the Tool.

That's what sets Dany apart: as well as being a respected industry leader and teacher, he has been able to take all that knowledge and experience and turn it into something practical: a machine that takes a client's financial information, digests it, and builds a personalized recipe for that client to optimize their finances through every stage of their working life and beyond. And because tax laws and investment mechanisms are constantly changing, and so are personal circumstances, we do this exercise regularly for each of our clients.

As the owner of a corporation, you could have three or four revenue streams, each taxed differently—for example, salary, dividend from your corporation, dividends from investments, and capital gains. Even comparing different investments and asset classes, the tax treatment can vary. For example, insurance and mutual fund assets are not taxed the same. Unfortunately, most modelling tools aren't programmed to that level of detail.

We go to great lengths to update The Tool every year as new rules and products hit the financial market. Of course, banks and other financial advice firms also have planning tools that are updated annually. In most cases, however, that simply means that they upload the latest tax bands. They keep the same broken paradigms they've always had because they're optimized for 95% of the market: T4 employees. Our Tool, on the other hand, is updated with new 'weapons' all the time, whether it be changes in the law, new financial instruments, or the realities of the market.

Every financial decision you make over the years should take into account four questions:

- What if I were to die today?
- What if I need this money early (or even right now)?
- What if I need this money in retirement?
- What if I need this money to pay taxes at death?

Using The Tool, we can model the financial impact of any upcoming decision, then vet and verify the output to make sure it makes sense. And if you bring us advice another professional gave you, we can also put that through the Tool to show you precisely what impact it will have on your finances. The Tool takes all the guesswork and misinformation out of everything we do. It allows us to account for the preferential tax treatment of one asset class over another, compare apples to apples, and translate everything into a common language: what will a strategy do to your investment returns, tax bill and total wealth?

The Tool is one of the only financial modelling tools optimized for corporations rather than T4 employees. The biggest gap in most models is in how they treat different revenue streams. Individuals and corporations are taxed differently—you know that. Otherwise, you wouldn't have incorporated! However, most tools ignore anything you leave inside the corporation: they only look at the money you take out of the corporation, and tax it as though it were T4 income.

A perfect example of the difference between The Tool and other models is in how they treat the Morneau Reforms. The reforms introduced incremental tax rates on passive investment income that start at $50,000 and increase in stages until, by the time that income reaches $150,000, you're paying tax at the maximum rate. All of this happened in 2018, and yet most tools haven't been updated yet to reflect how passive income inside a corporation will affect you as an independent consultant. Standard planning tools don't take the Morneau Reforms into account because the rules only apply to corporations, not private individuals—models optimized for T4 employees simply don't need to bother. As a result, most "consumer" financial planning models don't distinguish between income sources. Specifically, these tools

1. ignore whether income is passive or active
2. tax all income in a corporation at an average rate
3. usually only consider risk and gross rate of return.

Put these three factors together and, in an effort to reduce risk and fix income, a standard planning tool might suggest a strategy that earns lots of interest but ends up giving most of it to the taxman.

Which would you rather have: a strategy that gives you 15% taxed at 50% or one that gives you the same 15%, but tax-free?

When the Morneau Reforms were introduced, it took us a while, but we updated The Tool with all the details of the new regulations. So, when we're advising you where to put your money, we can say, "But don't put too much in there because you'll cross the next threshold, and your tax will be higher."

> I met with a potential client who is a CPA working as an Independent IT Consultant for big accounting firms. He'd already built a $2 Million portfolio in his corporation, and his attitude was, "I don't need you, Eric. I know what to do. I'm an accountant, and I can manage my own finances."
>
> As I dug deeper, though, he admitted he had a problem. "My portfolio makes $250,000 in passive income inside the corporation, and my tax bill makes my eyes water every year."

> So, I asked him, "If I come up with a solution that minimizes the tax burden on that passive income, would that be proof that you need me?" Of course, he became a client.

Maybe you don't have $2 Million in assets right now, and you're not making $250,000 in passive income. But the point is, we don't want you to get to the point where you are at that level, and because you didn't speak to us, you're paying too much tax!

Yes, the value of The Tool is in managing finances, coordinating action, and calculating factors that can't be worked out with a standard financial planning tool. But even more, it's about communication. I can show a client—even one who isn't financially savvy—the output, and they'll say, "That all makes sense. I didn't have the tools or knowledge to figure it out for myself, but now I see it on paper, I get it!" Many of them even say they never saw it that way before. Why? Because no one ever explained it to them from both sides of the equation at the same time: investment and taxation. But when I show them, they don't need a Ph.D. in finance to follow what I am saying.

Wondering whether you are properly set up for whatever the future may throw your way? We've created a simple online self-assessment that will model whether you're paying yourself too much, the tax impact of paying yourself dividends vs. salary, and other critical questions about how you manage your finances. To take the assessment, visit: https://consultant.financesti360.com/#net-worth-calculator-65yo

Chapter 4

The Three Phases of Your Financial Life

Every plan we build with a client sets the foundation for their financial prosperity across three phases of their life:

1. Accumulation
2. Withdrawal
3. Succession

Accumulation

The Accumulation phase is all about the science of growing your investments tax efficiently. In this phase, we put compounding into overdrive because the changes we make here will be in place for a long time, adding up year-on-year.

Withdrawal

The focus in the Withdrawal phase is taking your money out of your accounts (corporate and personal) tax-efficiently in retirement so that it provides the lifestyle you planned for without reducing the value of the pot. Not all withdrawal strategies are equal, and it's feasible to increase your retirement income by as much as 15-20% when you withdraw scientifically rather than following the standard (broken) withdrawal paradigm that most advisors recommend (you'll read more about that later in the book!).

Succession

The Succession phase is about ensuring that, at the end of your life, as much wealth as possible is transferred to your heirs rather than to the taxman. Importantly, however, we want you to have lived comfortably throughout your working life and retirement and done everything you wanted to do with your loved ones during your lifetime.

That is what sets us apart from other advisors you may have worked with. But don't get me wrong. We also ensure the CRA isn't left out or "cheated": the last thing you want is for the taxman to come after your family when you're gone, so we make sure CRA gets its fair share. We're not making enemies of the CRA with grey-hat (or worse, black-hat) tax strategies. We just ensure that you're only paying the taxes you have to and not a penny more. This is about tax *avoidance*, not tax *evasion*.

And believe it or not, minimizing your taxes is your constitutional right. It's in the Canadian Taxpayer Bill of Rights. Right #1 says, "You have the right to receive entitlements and to pay no more and no less than what is required by law. Under this right, you can expect to receive the benefits, credits, and refunds to which you are entitled under the law. You can also expect to pay no more and no less than the correct amount required under the law."[2] However, the only way you can exercise that right is by taking responsibility for determining precisely what "benefits, credits, and refunds" you're entitled to and the correct amount of tax you're "required" to pay.

We use The Tool (no great surprise!) to create financial plans in all three phases. But here's the important thing. It's not simply that The Tool can create a plan for the Accumulation phase, the Withdrawal phase, or the Succession phase. Dany designed The Tool from the ground up to coordinate everything *across* all three phases. It builds all three plans simultaneously and tracks the results of every decision. So, you can be sure you're not creating an Accumulation plan that's going to leave your family with nothing after you die or a Succession plan that will force you to scrimp and save in retirement in order to leave enough for your loved ones later.

[2] To ensure the currency and credibility of our information sources, and to obtain documentation supporting our assertions, please contact us at marketing@financesti360.com to access our references

Scarcity vs. Abundance

The financial world is set up to force you into a scarcity mindset: there's never enough. And if there's enough now, watch out! Because there might not be enough tomorrow.

That paradigm drives every aspect of how financial institutions and advisors do business. Usually, when you meet a new financial advisor, one of the first questions they'll ask you is how much money you've got, who you invest it with, and what rate of return you're getting. It's all about performance, and if you decide to work with them, they'll ask you to transfer everything to them: "Bring it to us, and we'll do better than your current investments."

Of course, the paradigm also shows up in how clients think. Most Independent Consultants spend their time and energy worrying about things like, "Am I putting enough into my pension plan? Am I putting in too much?" When we bring up the question of insurance, they always think they have more than enough—why should they put even more money into it? (They haven't figured out yet that it is an investment, not an expense). And, of course, the big question: What happens if I live longer than planned—will I run out of cash?"

In this part of the book, I'm going to get you to switch to an abundance mentality instead.

For many people, a major worry is what will happen if they live longer than planned: will they run out of cash?

There's an old saying in the medical profession: "Prescription without diagnosis is malpractice." The same applies to financial advice. We're not just trying to grow our funds under management—we don't get you to make any big decisions until both of us have all the information needed. The critical point is that, for us, onboarding a new client isn't about saying you should let us look after all your money because we'll do a better job than your current advisors. Instead, it's about helping you feel encouraged, confident, and empowered to make decisions for yourself and feel confident saying, "OK, let's do this!"

Now, different people use different words and ask different questions, but everyone is looking for "The Recipe." Well, I can't give you a recipe, because there is no one-size-fits-all strategy. That's why we use The Tool: it shows the financial logic behind every decision. That way, no investment is ever made based on "let's just put a little more in here to be safe."

In our initial meetings, we will be getting to know you, so while we might make suggestions and observations, our focus is on asking questions and looking for evidence that you might be following some broken paradigms. That can range from the basics, like whether you pay yourself a salary or take dividends, to issues that might be more specific to you.

We take notes on everything you say and feed it into The Tool so that we can let you know what we need to focus on in future meetings. With that information, we can start to help you use your money differently: more efficiently to minimize tax and more effectively to maximize revenue.

By the second meeting, we will bring specific advice and solutions. Even then, we're not just looking for one-for-one trades ("Our RRSP is better than the one you have. So, let's switch you over."). Instead, we're far more likely to suggest a completely different vehicle that is better suited to your needs as an Independent Consultant and business owner.

IT360 Financial is like a buffet: we bring everything at our disposal to the table, but it's your choice what you take advantage of. It's your plan. We build it together to minimize tax and maximize revenue, but I want you to understand all the moving parts. I want you to know how everything fits together and, most importantly, to be able to tell the difference between "good" advice and great advice.

Ultimately, we want you to feel that you're in control of your financial future, choosing the strategies that make the most sense for you. We're not a black box you put your money into and hope for the best. So, we bring you recommendations and show you the impact of each option (using the Tool), but you get to make all the significant choices with our guidance and direction.

The Accumulation Phase

Chapter 5

Starting up

The Accumulation phase is all about growing your investments tax-efficiently. That should start the day you set up your business. Most consultants set up their company, trade through it, and keep it until the day they die. They're not building a business to sell on; it is simply a holding company to accumulate wealth. After they retire, they withdraw the money until either there's none left or they die. So, if the company is just a vehicle for building and storing your wealth, it makes sense to do everything possible to maximize the value you're generating.

Generally, there are three kinds of people who become Independent Consultants.

1. Employees looking for something they feel is missing from employment (be that control, money, variety, or whatever).
2. Late career professionals who want to leverage their knowledge in retirement.
3. Graduates who don't want to just disappear into the corporate meat grinder.

Let's look at those groups in turn: what drives them, what can hold them back, and what's important in planning their financial future.

1. The Employee

The first is an employee who one day realizes that many of his colleagues are Independent Consultants. Inevitably, they start comparing things like hourly rates and lifestyle, and it's not long before the employee begins to wonder how hard it would be to set up a business themselves. After all, they know they have the skills, and they're just as good as the next guy, so why not?

That leads to three inevitable questions.

1. How will I get contracts?
2. How hard is it to set up a corporation?
3. How do I make sure I'll have money in retirement? How will I cope without my retirement plan?

Getting contracts as an IT consultant can be easier than you expect. Many IT consultants start their career working for their former employer. Others draw on the personal contacts and relationships they've built over the course of their career. However, one of the simplest and fastest ways to get started can be to sign up with an agency. They exist to build relationships with IT employers, and they are constantly watching the market for opportunities to connect their consultants to potential hirers.

The best agencies put their consultants at the centre of their decision-making and work hard to match them with the best contracts based on their expertise and experience. Of course, there are good and bad agencies. One way to protect yourself and ensure that you are working with a good agency is to look for a member of the National Association of Canadian Consulting Businesses. NACCB is a professional body that brings together 75 major staffing firms across Canada (including Cofomo, Randstad, and Procom), representing over 100,000

Independent Consultants. Working with an NACCB member gives you the reassurance that your agency is following industry standards and guidelines.

Similarly, setting up a company can be much easier than you think if you partner with someone who creates corporations for a living and focuses on working with Independent Consultants. At the same time, just because something is easy doesn't mean it's simple, which is why you need to work with experts who do this every day.

That leaves retirement: how can you optimize your situation in every way possible to ensure you don't run out of money later in life and can support the lifestyle you want in retirement? The problem here isn't just making sure you have enough. It's also about investing tax-efficiently. If you don't know what you're doing, or you follow the same strategies you had as a T4 employee, it is very easy to invest your money in ways that will end up costing you more tax later.

2. The Late-Career Professional

The second type of person who typically becomes an Independent Consultant is someone who has had a successful career (usually in a big corporation or the public sector) and starts consulting in retirement. Like the Employee above, these professionals are also worried about how hard it might be to set up a corporation—and the answer is the same: find a professional who focuses on creating companies for Independent Consultants, and work with an agency that is a member of NACCB.

Unlike the Employee, however, they're often not too worried about finding contracts initially. After all, this person was already wealthy enough to retire. Eventually, however, even the Late-Career

Professional will want more work, and an agency can be a great help here. Many of these late-stage professionals also have another, much better problem: "What should I do with all this money?" Unlike the Employee, they're generally not worried about running out of cash. Their conversation with us is more likely to go something like, "I'm getting $175,000 a year in pension, I'm billing $200,000 through my corporation, and now I've got this extra income from my portfolio. How do I get my money out tax-efficiently?"

If you don't know what you're doing in that situation, it's easy to end up paying much more tax now than you need to.

3. The Graduate

In recent years, a third type of person has entered the contracting market: recent graduates who leave university and realize they don't want to be an employee. Not long ago, it was unusual for someone to go straight from university into independent consulting. You needed one or two grey hairs before considering that path because, unless you had at least five or ten years of experience, none of the major agencies or employers would look at you for a consulting position. However, staffing shortages in the industry have made it easier for new entrants to come straight in and create financial success early in their professional career (and if you're still in college or university and reading this, then you should at least consider it as a career option).

Of course, new graduates have the same doubts and challenges about setting up a corporation as more experienced consultants. However, for them, the critical piece is getting their first contract—which makes it even more essential to find a good agency.

Getting Started

Setting up in business is a manic time, with lots to do. Your top priority must be to incorporate, which brings significant benefits. Operating as a company limits your personal risk and liability. More importantly, a corporation is an excellent investment vehicle with substantial tax advantages and—critically—ensures that your business can continue to exist after your death and shelter your investments.

Once you've registered your business name, obtained a business number, and registered for sales taxes, your next priority is to find the right professionals to guide you. You'll need an accountant to prepare your annual financial statements, file your business income and sales tax returns, and prepare your tax paperwork (T4/T5 for salaries, R1/R3 for dividends). Along with an accountant, you'll need a bookkeeper and someone to process and report your payroll. Your accountant or bookkeeper will also help you create balance sheets and profit and loss accounts throughout the year, budgets and forecasts, and a cash flow analysis. They'll also track how things change from month to month and how you're performing against budget. Next on the list is an attorney who knows business law so they can help you review your contracts. That means the lawyer who helped you buy your house probably isn't going to cut it!

But the Accumulation phase isn't just about taking care of admin matters. As you've probably figured out by now, where we really help is in minimizing taxation and maximizing revenue. So, along with the experts I listed above, you'll also need an excellent financial planner. They are the key to making the most of the Accumulation phase, protecting your family finances, planning for retirement, and tracking and analyzing your portfolio. Finally, you'll need to find a great insurance broker and a tax advisor who understand the intricacies of working with Independent Consultants.

Tax Status

Regardless of why someone becomes an Independent Consultant and where they are in their career, one of their biggest concerns is usually around tax status: how do you ensure that CRA will accept that you truly are an independent business owner? Because if they don't, you'll be treated as an employee and lose all the tax advantages you should be enjoying.

The challenge here is that the guidelines (and they are very much guidelines rather than fixed rules) vary by province and change over time. Worse still, they are subject to interpretation by CRA on a case-by-case basis[3]. All of this creates a lot of fear, uncertainty, and doubt for Independent Consultants. So, the only way to ensure you don't make an expensive misstep is to talk to someone like IT360 Financial. We make it our business to stay up to date with evolving regulations and practices across the country, and we work closely with accountants and lawyers across Canada who regularly deal with CRA to defend consultants in tax investigations and appeals.

Despite everything I just said, however, there are some easy steps you can take that can't guarantee you'll be seen as independent but will strengthen your case. We've already mentioned, for example, the importance of disability insurance as an indicator that you are running

---

[3] https://www.canada.ca/en/revenue-agency/services/tax/canada-pension-plan-cpp-employment-insurance-ei-rulings/cpp-ei-explained/canada-pension-plan-employment-insurance-explained-information-technology-consultants-employees-self-employed-workers.html

a 'real' business. Other critical insurances you need are Errors and Omissions Insurance and General Liability Insurance, which cover you if you do something that causes loss or harm to your client.

Losing your tax status can be an expensive mistake. Don't take risks with your financial situation. That's why we've created a simple tool to check your status based on your answers to a few critical questions.

Check your tax status for free at

https://consultant.financesti360.com/#validate-tax-status

Getting The Right Financial Advice

Your advisors' goal should be to optimize your tax situation, identify the best way to withdraw money from the corporation while you're still working, and reduce your income taxes now and in retirement. That provides a straightforward test of the value of the advice you're getting, as there are three more common Broken Paradigms when it comes to taking money out for your day-to-day needs, and they have a significant impact on your taxes and revenue.

Broken Paradigm #2: Salary vs. Dividends

A critical question you face each year throughout your career as an Independent Consultant is whether to take money out as salary or dividend. It's impossible to answer that correctly without looking at the long-term implications of your choice. So, it's not a question that your accountant can answer on their own because they don't have the tools to model those implications accurately.

If you do ask, your accountant will probably say you should take a dividend because "It's simpler, and the tax is roughly the same." That's true if you only consider the impact over a single tax year. And for an accountant, that's a reasonable basis for the answer. You probably didn't ask them about the long term, and even if you look one to five years into the future, the difference between payroll and dividend is likely to be small. However, if they were to model salary vs. dividend over multiple decades—say 20, 30, or 40 years into the future—the difference would be significant: when you retire, you could be tens of thousands of dollars a year worse off.

Most new consultants ask the question when they first set up their business, but very few revisit it further down the line. So even if your accountant's advice would be different today, you'll probably never know. But almost every time a client's accountant has an opportunity to talk to us, they change their mind.

The real answer is, "It depends." It varies from province to province and based on personal circumstances. It also changes over time as tax laws and rates change. Importantly, though, paying yourself dividends in the Accumulation phase closes off a lot of other tax optimization strategies available if you pay yourself a salary. And because everything changes from year to year, the decision needs to be reviewed regularly.

Broken Paradigm #3: Income Splitting When You Shouldn't

Another potential minefield for the unwary business owner is income splitting: "moving" income to your spouse because they are in a lower bracket than you.

> For example, assume your wife made $50,000 in taxable income for 2021, and you took $250,000 out of the corporation as taxable income. In Ontario, your wife would have paid $7,657 in income tax, and you'd have paid $95,084—between you, you paid over $102,000 in personal income tax.
>
> With income splitting, you would instead pay yourself $150,000 and the other $100,000 to your wife (raising her taxable income to $150,000, too). In Ontario in 2021, the tax on $150,000 was $45,159. So, your combined income tax bill would have been just over $90,000, saving about $12,000.

On the face of it, income splitting seems a great idea and a convenient way to reduce your taxes. For many years it was a very useful tool in the Accumulation phase, and many advisors still recommend it. The problem is that you can only pass income to a spouse or adult child if they are investing in the business or doing significant work for it. So, if your spouse is a housewife or working full-time in another job, you can't just hand them the money to save tax. And if you've been doing that, you're sitting on a ticking time bomb. If CRA suspects you're incorrectly income splitting, that can trigger an audit and open you up to a reassessment of past tax years, with accompanying penalties and interest. Fortunately, the regulations don't apply once you're over 65, so income splitting is still useful in the Withdrawal phase: once you reach retirement age, you can pay dividends however you like from the company, even if you're still working.

> One of my clients is 68 and still working full time as an Independent Consultant. He pays his wife a $50,000 dividend, and the tax man has no problem with it, even though she's retired.

Broken Paradigm #4: Assessing Risk Tolerance

Risk tolerance is about assessing how much risk you are willing to accept in your investments. Unfortunately, the way most finance professionals discuss this is flawed. The standard approach asks the wrong questions and ignores context. So, when we ask a potential client about their risk tolerance, they'll say something like, "I did a questionnaire with my guy, and he told me I'm a Growth Investor: I'm willing to take some risks, but I won't gamble everything."

Here's the thing: The way risk tolerance is usually assessed ends up putting 95% of respondents in that category because people's overall attitudes to risk fall on a bell curve. While there are a few "cowboys" who love taking risks and a few "turtles" who hate it, the majority fall somewhere in the middle. And because everyone ends up in the same risk category, and all asset categories get treated the same way, everyone gets broadly similar advice:

1. Put your money into your RRSP
2. When you reach your RRSP limit, put it into your TFSA
3. When you've maxed out your RRSP and TFSA, build a portfolio (following the same risk profile)

This happens because the questions asked are too broad—they're looking at general financial risk tolerance—and the replies are applied uniformly to every aspect of the client's investments. Instead, the advisor should be drilling down on the client's risk tolerance for specific categories of investment, like registered accounts (TFSA,

RRSP, etc.), open accounts (their corporate portfolio), etc. But that's not the end of it. Because most people are in the same risk category, they end up with the same portfolio, even though they think it's tailored to their personal risk profile: the Growth Portfolio

- 30% in fixed-income investments (which currently generate around 2% annual return)
- 70% in stocks (which average around 10% return).

As we saw in Chapter 2, this 'average' portfolio returns 7% per annum, and the income isn't treated the same when it comes to taxation. As a reminder, interest income from bonds is taxed at up to 50%. Meanwhile, income from stocks gets much more favourable treatment. Dividends you receive from investments are taxed at preferential rates, and in some cases, you can even recover part of the tax you pay on dividends from Canadian corporations. Later, when you sell the shares, Capital Gains Tax only applies to 50% of any gain.[4]

So, as we've already said, holding fixed-income investments will protect you from falling markets, but it comes at a high cost. I prefer to look at risk in a different way. Let's say you have a $1 million portfolio in your corporation, and your advisor structured it as a growth portfolio with 30% bonds and 70% stocks. But then you come to us, and I ask, "Why do you have 30% of your portfolio in fixed-income investments?"

"Because my advisor suggested it as a way to mitigate risk. He told me it's like a parachute: if the market falls, my total portfolio will only go down by 50% of the drop."

---

[4] See also https://taxsummaries.pwc.com/canada/corporate/income-determination and https://hillnotes.ca/2021/11/02/corporate-income-taxes-in-canada-revenue-rates-and-rationale-2/

Now I know that what you really want is a safety net. That's a critical point because now we're looking for something that acts like a fixed-income investment but won't get taxed as interest. And, as I said in Chapter 2, this is where insurance comes into the picture: look below the surface, and insurance acts like a fixed-income investment product in many respects. Savvy advisors who are used to working with business owners know the magic this strategy can do for a business.

You need to work with the 1% of advisors who can see that.

> As a side note, many investors don't really understand the idea of "fixed income." A common mistake is thinking that "fixed" is the same as guaranteed. It doesn't. Fixed income just means that you can predict with a high degree of confidence what your return will be. It's more certain than a stock, but it's not guaranteed—and in 2022, fixed-income investments actually gave negative returns!

With that in mind, instead of putting part of your portfolio into fixed-income investments at a low rate of return (and paying 50% tax on that!), we'll put that money into specialized insurance products and get a much higher return tax-efficiently. Then what do we do with the rest? Well, that depends again on your risk tolerance. The mistake many advisors (and clients) make is assuming it's still the same as it was at the start of the process: you're in the middle of the curve, looking for moderate risk.

But remember that a significant part of your portfolio is now invested in a low-risk, fixed-income product. So, you can be more aggressive with the rest, and your *overall* risk profile will still be in line with the old 30/70 portfolio. The real goal is to create a portfolio that acts like the 30/70 portfolio you want, but where each component has a different role to play. Some assets will be higher risk, and others will be lower, but overall, the portfolio honours your risk tolerance. The way we would achieve that in IT360 Financial is by creating a Corporate Investment Policy for you built around that objective.

Broken Paradigm #5: Setting RRSP Contributions

Many advisors say, "Max out your RRSP contributions," but they can't prove that's the best course of action. As we saw earlier, with an RRSP, your contributions are capped, you're paying contributions out of post-tax income, and your management fees aren't tax deductible. What you need is something that acts like an RRSP but isn't capped, is paid for out of pre-tax income and has deductible management fees. That's why IT360 Financial teamed up with one of Canada's largest pension plan groups to create the E-PP that you read about in Chapter 2: a product that is simple to set up and manage, that acts like an RRSP but allows you to put in up to 30% of your salary or T-4 income (depending on age), where the contributions are tax deductible for the corporation, and so are the fees.

Before you launch your career as an independent professional, ensure you're set up to take full advantage of the benefits of incorporation. The biggest question we get from new independent consultants is, "Should I incorporate?" We've created a **short** online self-assessment so you can answer that question for yourself. To take the assessment, visit:

https://consultant.financesti360.com/#incorporationornot

Case Study 2

The Independent Expert: Vlad Catrinescu

Being an Independent Consultant isn't always about going from company to company, contract to contract, completing projects. Microsoft MVP Vlad Catrinescu from Montreal, Canada, started consulting while still a student. He has gone on to build a successful international career as an author, speaker, trainer, and consultant on SharePoint and Microsoft 365. Long before COVID-19 forced companies to "go virtual," Vlad was helping organizations to get set up for remote working.

I've always been passionate about computers. I often joke that I'm "second-generation SharePoint" because my dad was also a SharePoint expert—in fact, he was the one who got me into the industry when I was just 18. Then I went to college to do a computer science degree, and halfway through the program, I started consulting.

Like many Independent Consultants, I started with short-term contracts for local clients: you get a gig for six months, and when that ends, you have to find another one. However, I very quickly realized that model wasn't scalable. There are only 24 hours in a day, and you can't work all those hours: you need to sleep sometime!

So, I asked myself, "How can I turn 'Vlad' into a service and leverage that? The answer was that I started creating content for an online training platform called Pluralsight, and by the end of the year, I hope to be on several other platforms. The great thing is I only need to record lessons once, and people can watch them whenever they want. I'm also an author, with three books published by Apress.

That shift is what has allowed me to scale my business and get known all over the world. That works for me because I love to travel. Before the Pandemic, I used to travel about 150 days a year, speaking at conferences across the globe in places like Australia, Sri Lanka, and all over Europe. In the first half of 2022, I got to go to Berlin, Las Vegas, and Cancun. It's hard to say no to beautiful places like those, especially when the conference covers most of your travel costs!

Even before I became an Independent Consultant, I had always worked for consultancies. My first job after college was in internal IT for a consulting firm. I ended up moving into a consulting role in the same company, and after a while, I moved to another consulting company, which was how I ended up going independent!

My new employers had trouble selling me. They had a whole team dedicated to SharePoint, but they couldn't get me a project, so I spent all summer "on the bench." After three months of that, I was climbing the walls. So, I asked my boss, "Can I just go out and find my own contracts?"

"Sure," he said. "Knock yourself out!"

Two days later, I came back with a contract.

After that, I got my Microsoft MVP[5] status, and I started to get itchy feet. As I said above, I love to travel, and being an employee severely limited my ability to travel and attend conferences: consulting companies want you to be billable for as much of your time as possible, not sitting in a hotel watching keynotes.

Even though I was only 23, I decided it was time to strike out on my own. I had no dependents, so if it all went wrong, no one would get hurt; I might end up living in my parents' basement, but at least I could say I'd tried.

It helped that I was a Microsoft MVP with experience in consulting. I even had sales experience—as a teen, I'd worked in a store selling laptops, TVs, etc. And I'd proved I could sell my own services by getting that contract (and if I was going to have to go out and find clients anyway, why not get them for myself and keep all the money rather than give it to a company and only get a fraction of it!).

As an Independent Consultant, I am master of my own time. I don't have a boss looking over my shoulder asking why my billable time is down this week or telling me when I can or can't take a vacation. I get to choose which events I will attend (and if there's a specific place I want to travel to, I can look for events there!), and often, they turn into a mini vacation—I'm not going to fly to Europe just for a day. So, I usually add a few days on either side of an event to enjoy the location.

Of course, there are downsides to everything, even life as an Independent Consultant. At the end of the day, you're responsible for yourself, which is both the biggest advantage and the biggest

---

5 *Most Valued Professional ("MVP") is an award given by Microsoft to only 3,000 people across the globe.*

disadvantage. And there's a lot to take care of. You have to have one eye on future strategy—what do I want the business to look like in one year? And in five? Do I still want to look for contracts? Do I want to create a product?—and at the same time, you have to take care of the present and ensure you're looking after the clients you've got.

You also have to deal with a lot of uncertainty. Sometimes you don't know whether a client will renew, and increasingly, clients insist on short-term renewable contracts. A few years ago, you might only have faced that uncertainty once a year, but now it comes around every three months.

> Note from Eric: It's not only you who has to learn to be comfortable with uncertainty: your family and dependents will also be feeling the pressure. It's important to think about that and discuss it openly with your loved ones when deciding whether contracting is the right path for you.

Those shorter contracts add an extra level of pressure, too. If you start a 12-month project in March, you know that barring a major change, it will renew next March, and if it doesn't, Spring isn't a bad time to be looking for a contract. But if the contract is only for three months, it could end in June. That's a terrible time to be looking for a new gig because not many major projects kick off between June and September. So, you could be on the bench all summer.

Remember, also, that as an Independent Consultant, you're not just an IT worker but a business owner. In fact, you are chief shareholder, CEO, CIO, CMO, COO, and pretty much every other CXO, including CCO (Chief Coffee Officer)! That means you have to take care of sales and marketing, and you need to understand accounting (even if you hire a bookkeeper and an accountant) and finance (even if you have a financial planner). You need to know enough to ask the right questions, understand the answers and recommendations you get, and make informed decisions.

And even if you are with clients 40 or more hours a week, you need to make time for your business responsibilities. Otherwise, they don't get done. I've even known other consultants who would forget to do the invoicing for several months, which I find hard to believe. Sending an invoice is the best part of being a business owner! (OK, second best—the best part is when that invoice gets paid!).

All of that means that the early years can be stressful. However, once things settle down and you've built up a good nest egg in the bank, it becomes very rewarding and liberating.

In the early days, I depended on agencies to get clients for me, but I'm not a fan of that approach. They're great when you're starting out because they handle the relationship with the client and make sure you get paid. Also, many big corporations outsource hiring consultants to those agencies, so they're sometimes the only route to the big jobs until you get well-known in your industry.

These days, however, I get my own contracts. Even though I live in Montreal, I tend to look for clients outside the province because rates are much higher in the US, Western Canada, and other places than in Quebec. And the difference can be huge. In Quebec, if you tell a company you're looking for $120 an hour, they'll tell you you're crazy. But you can go to someone in California and say you want $250 an hour, and they'll jump at it.

Even better, much of my work can be performed remotely, so I can sit in Quebec earning California rates. Before COVID, some clients were less open to having a consultant working virtually, but since the

Pandemic, it's become normal. And that means that as an Independent Consultant, you can work with clients anywhere in the world.

I started working with IT360 Financial in 2018. At that point, I'd already been in business for a few years, and I had an accountant to file my taxes and accounts. Also, my mom works in HR, so she advised me on setting up things like payroll. Apart from them, however, Eric was the first professional advisor I hired. Before that, I hadn't even spoken to an insurance agent about things like Critical Illness—I just took out the policies my professional association recommended. These days, I have three policies just as investments!

The problem I found trying to get good advice was that when you search online, it's all really about marketing. I didn't want someone to tell me what I *could* do or what *might* work for me: I wanted an advisor who would say, "Do this. Now do this." So, it definitely helps to work with somebody who focuses on helping business owners and does this every day. For one thing, I'm not burning billable hours going down internet rabbit holes trying to find good advice.

If I were talking to a potential client, I'd say something like, "Look, are you going to give this job to someone in your IT department who's never done it before, but they'll read a book and watch some YouTube videos? Or are you going to hire me because this is all I do, I do it every day, and I've done it many times? Of course, you'll pay me more, but you know the job will get done right the first time."

For me, hiring Eric is just the same. And I also know that if I get any questions from my accountant, CRA, or whoever, I can just forward them to Eric and his team, and they'll probably know the answer.

Working with IT360 Financial has completely changed how I manage my finances. I'm doing many things I didn't even know were possible. For instance, I mentioned that my mom advised me on setting up my company. But that's not the only way she has helped my business. Working with Eric, I took out a life insurance policy on my parents (which, obviously, I hope I won't claim on for a very long time). As a result, I'll get a $1 Million payout tax-free when they're both gone.

That's crazy because usually, to make a million dollars net, you have to earn two or three times that amount before tax. I would never have come up with that idea if Eric hadn't suggested it. And it took a lot of paperwork, but IT360 Financial prepared most of it for me. All I had to do was read it and sign on the dotted line.

Retirement is still a long way off for me, but I've always liked the idea of going into semi-retirement one day. Right now, I'm young with no kids or even a dog, and I love what I do. So, I work way more than 40 hours a week. But I also know it's much easier to do that when you're young, and I can't keep that up forever, or I won't be here to enjoy the money I made!

So, I'm looking forward to reaching an age—and I'm sure Eric will use The Tool to tell me exactly what age that will be—where I can slow down and semi-retire. I'll take a project here and there to keep active and not get bored, and if I want to take six months off to go travelling, I can. But, for now, I'll hustle and save money so I can retire early and enjoy life (while I can still do crazy things that maybe I won't be able to do when I'm older!).

That's the joy of being financially independent: you reach a point where you work because you love it, not because you must.

Ultimately, there is so much you don't know about, and it would take too long to study every subject and understand it. The alternative is to work with a team like Eric's, who have seen many different consultants and can advise the best course of action based on your age, financial status, and other factors.

Yes, you could do the research yourself, but why bother when they take care of all that for you? Focus on what you do best, which is IT consulting, rather than trying to become a financial advisor and accountant all at the same time. Let someone who's an expert in what they do take care of that instead.

Chapter 6

The Fork in the Road

At some point in your contracting career, you'll face a decision: do you keep on the path, or do you return to the warm embrace of permanent employment?

For many, the choice is obvious: "I'm never going back." Some consultants love the benefits of being independent: they feel that, at last, they're in control of their life, making money and comfortable with their finances. For them, the big question is, "When can I retire?" The decision comes down to a choice between retiring richer or retiring sooner: every year they work means more money available for retirement. So, the real question is, how much money are you willing to forego tomorrow for freedom today? And if you retire today, will you have enough money to see you through a longer retirement?

That's not as easy to answer as it seems. It's about how much money you want to have in retirement and whether you'll be able to sustain your lifestyle, not knowing how long you'll live after retirement. And the decision isn't just about money. Some consultants just say to themselves, "**** it. I've done a lot better than I thought I would. It's time to enjoy myself." But if you stop working at 58, what will you do in retirement? If you've been a business owner, you're probably not someone who would be happy sitting on a balcony every day watching the world pass you by. So, do you have another plan? Could you semi-retire and work six months a year, or perhaps live abroad and work remotely?

"If the right offer comes my way..."

Other consultants are nervous about committing to their career long-term and stay open to going back to being an employee. On the one hand, there are worries about hitting a "dry patch" if a contract ends and they can't get a new one. On the other, there's the worry that if they do go back, they might not enjoy salaried life—but at the same time, there's no guarantee that they'll always love life as an Independent Consultant. And of course, while all this is going through the consultant's mind, there is one other factor to consider: employers are making more and better offers all the time.

Why go back?

Ultimately, consultants go back to being T4 employees for five main reasons.

1. Money
2. Lifestyle
3. To strengthen their résumé
4. Promotion
5. Security

Let's look at the reality of each of those reasons.

Money

Some are seduced by the perceived financial benefits of employment, like access to group insurance, a pension plan, or paid vacation. It's easy to make the wrong decision if you don't talk to an advisor first. Maybe you'll get group insurance worth $3,000 per year, company pension contributions of 7-8%, and eight weeks of paid vacation. But it may not compensate for the rate cut you'll have to take. Also, more benefits without your corporate "shelter" could mean more taxes to pay. When you work the numbers, you might find that you'll actually be $20,000 worse off! That's why we model everything with The Tool: so we can compare apples to apples.

Lifestyle

Even if the money is worse, you might still decide to go back because of lifestyle and other intangibles. Maybe you'll be working closer to home, or you simply believe life will be much simpler working for someone else. That's a trade-off, and only you can decide whether it's worth it—but make sure you choose with full knowledge of all the factors. You'll need to have a conversation with your significant other, and you'll need to put a dollar value on everything because, in the end, the real question you're considering is how much money you are willing to give up for those lifestyle benefits.

Résumé Building

Others return to being an employee to acquire marketable expertise. It's hard to learn new skills and experience as an Independent Consultant. From that perspective, taking a "permanent" role is a smart move (of course, no job is ever permanent, and you can always go back to contracting down the line). You get to do your professional development on someone else's dime and get paid while you build your experience. So, you go back to being an employee for 18 to 24 months, and then you come back as an Independent Consultant commanding a higher rate: it's taking one step back to take two steps forward.

Promotion

Another reason for going back can be promotion. In the past, it was hard for a consultant to get to sit in the VP or CIO's chair. Today, however, there's a severe staffing shortage in IT, so the top roles are open even to consultants. The reality is that wanting a management position is no longer a good reason to go back to being an employee.

Security

Of course, one of the biggest reasons consultants leave the independent life is the perceived security of a corporate job. It's easy to assume that being an employee brings more job security. While that may have been true in the past, there are no jobs for life anymore. When there's work for everyone, and you're good at your job, you get to keep it. And if you're bad at what you do, it doesn't matter whether you're an employee or a consultant: you will get fired! On the other hand, while it's easy to get fired by an employer, you'll never fire yourself.

"But Eric," you say. "Aren't consultants the first people to be let go when things get shaky? Maybe I can't get sacked by an employer, but a client can terminate a contract." Here's the thing. Even when the economy is down, employers don't just fire all the consultants and keep the employees. Consultants are often brought in because of specialized skills and typically have more experience and knowledge than permanent employees, often gained across multiple sectors.

For example, many of our consultants have moved between industries—private and retail banking, the insurance sector, hydro, and the public sector. People with that sort of cross-industry experience bring expertise that simply cannot be bought. So, a CIO will think very carefully before firing all the consultants.

Broadening your experience is the best way to remain relevant in your career because it keeps you at the top of your game, bringing to the table best practices from other industries and employers. On the other hand, when someone has been with the same company for 15 or 20 years, they get stuck in old paradigms. And the longer they stay in their chair, the more irrelevant and narrow-minded they become.

The Big Question

Ultimately, the question is whether you are better off as a consultant or an employee. But to answer that, you need to figure out exactly what "better off" means to you. And in order to decide, you have to make sure you have all the *facts* you need. The only way to make up your mind is to know all the facts and work with someone who knows the ins and outs and can do a thorough analysis. But that's not the financial planner at your bank, your accountant, or the tax advisor in the local strip mall.

Before you make a major decision with long-term implications for your finances, contact us, and we'll model the impact of your options. Schedule a meeting with one of our professional advisors to discuss your plans and avoid expensive mistakes. To get started, visit

https://consultant.financesti360.com/#book-a-meeting

Case Study 3

The Boomerang Consultant: Rémi Lafrance

One of the big things to bear in mind about becoming an Independent Consultant is that it isn't a one-way street: you always have the option to go back. Some, like Ghislaine, who you'll read about in Case Study 6, take a full-time salaried role to advance their career; others consider each new opportunity—whether salaried or a contract position—and pick the ones they want.

The important thing is that if you decide to return to being an employee—whether permanently or only temporarily—you must make sure you don't lose all the advantages you enjoy thanks to the time you spent as a consultant. Rémi Lafrance is an excellent example of someone who has gone back and forth between contracting and T4 status but works with us to ensure he doesn't lose the tax benefits he accrued as an independent.

I started life as an electrical engineer, and I'm also a musician—so I have complementary competencies: I can speak numbers and Cartesian logic, but I'm also creative and innovative. It's a combination the market is crying out for these days.

I've been in digital transformation forever, working on some of the most significant projects in that field. I started at CBC in the 80s, helping them switch to digital broadcasting. Then, during the Y2K 'panic,' I was an Independent Consultant.

When the dust settled after the millennium, I got an offer that was hard to refuse from Aeroplan, so I took the leap back into being an employee and stayed there for almost 20 years. Eventually, I got itchy feet and wanted to be my own boss again, so I took a short contracting gig at CN (where I met Eric). Then I got another of those hard-to-refuse opportunities to become CIO for Exo (the company that runs mass transit in Montréal suburbs), so I went back to being an employee for three years.

When I felt I'd taken that role as far as I could, I sat back and weighed up various opportunities. Some were a chance to go back to being a consultant; others were salaried positions. In the end, the most appealing role was as VP of the Digital Solutions Center for Alithya, a major Canadian digital transformation consultancy. They have acquired a lot of smaller firms over recent years and needed help to bring everything together. So, right now, I'm an employee again, and I'll probably go back to consulting in a few years as I get closer to retirement.

There are upsides and downsides to both contracting and employment, and my way of working has given me access to both.

Consultants enjoy a lot of freedom. You can take a contract for as long as you want, and you get to negotiate on your own terms. If you want to take a month or two off between projects, you can. On top of that, of course, there are all the tax advantages of incorporation (which, thanks to Eric, I now know more about than I ever did before!). Inside a company, you have much more control over how your money is managed. So, you can make the best use of it, with many options that simply don't exist for employees.

On a professional growth level, also, you can move from client to client, looking for new challenges, or you can specialize, and people hire you for that one thing.

The downside, however, is that external consultants don't always get a seat at the table, especially for big strategic decisions. That's something I've always hated because I love to be at the heart of decision-making, identifying solutions for the future, driving transformation and helping the organization to grow. That's not typically part of a consultant's remit unless you're explicitly hired as a strategy consultant—and that kind of gig comes later in your career when you have more experience. More often, you're hired to do a specific job, and that's what you do. So, whenever I've been a consultant, I've felt left out of things, and that's been a big incentive to become part of the company and get a seat at the table.

Working with Eric, I have organized my financial affairs to take full advantage of corporate status. As an employee, I don't enjoy the same benefits, but I wanted to be sure that when I went back to being a salaried employee, I wouldn't have to lose the financial advantages I'd earned as a consultant. Fortunately, IT360 Financial has shown me how to keep growing the money inside my corporation even if I can't add to it while I'm an employee.

That's another reason I want to go back to being an Independent Consultant before I retire: to put as much value as possible into the corporate pot to fund my retirement and to leave to my family. That's much smarter than simply maxing out my RRSP. I started my career at CBC in the eighties when no one talked about RRSPs. When I left CBC, I had many years' worth of RRSP contribution headroom that I hadn't used. As a result, I missed out on decades of compound interest and growth on those unused contributions. And because the CBC pension was a defined-benefit plan, I'd never had to think about risk management. Now, that's something I watch very carefully, thanks to Eric. The way IT360 Financial thinks about risk is very different from other advisors. They're not aiming to be the first to buy or sell, but they ensure they're not late to the party. They don't take as many risks as some other portfolio managers, and in the long term, it has certainly paid off for me because they're always there at the right time, making the right moves, selling when it's time to sell and buying when it's time to buy.

That timing can have a massive impact on your investments. For example, when my Y2K contract finished, I was working with a financial planner who had made some great investments for me. Unfortunately, he held onto them way too long, and they lost a lot of value when the tech bubble burst a few years later. It wasn't a disaster, but it could have turned out a lot better than it did.

I'm a strong advocate of working with the best to get the most out of the critical decisions you need to make in your life. For example, when I left Exo, I hired a couple of executive coaches to help me think through what I wanted to do with the rest of my career. After losing out on many years of RRSP contributions and compound growth and having my fingers burned after the tech bubble burst, I appreciated the importance of getting professional advice. That's when I realized I needed to take things much more seriously.

When it comes to finances, you're dealing with significant sums of money, and you need to think straight about how best to use those investments. So, it makes sense to work with the best and get inspired by how they do things. How do they plan disbursements? How do they use insurance to cover the taxes on whatever will be left? These are questions I would never have thought about on my own.

As I mentioned, I met Eric when I left Aeroplan in 2018—that's when I set up my company and hired an accountant who suggested I talk to IT360 Financial. At the time, I had been working with a financial advisor for many years, but it quickly became apparent he didn't have anything like the same depth of insight and experience when it came to dealing with Independent Consultants rather than salaried employees. He didn't have the same understanding of the future implications of the decisions I was making and how they would affect disbursements—we'd never even talked about disbursements!—or how the things I'd done in the past were going to affect my finances in the future (and what we should do about it).

By comparison, my conversations with IT360 Financial were much more insightful and valuable. For example, my wife took maternity leave around 2010, and we didn't make any contributions to her pension. When I started working with Eric, we discussed whether it made sense to buy back those missing years and the impact it would have in the short and long term.

Meeting Eric was a game-changer for me. After realizing my mistake at CBC (not using my RRSP allowance), I had made sure to put money in every year. During my 18 years at Aeroplan, I maxed out my RRSP. But then I met Eric, and I wished I'd had his help sooner. Because he would have helped me figure out the best place to put everything to make use of all those dollars, consolidate my assets, and start thinking about disbursements.

Recently, Eric and I used The Tool to model my retirement and see how things will unfold: what money my wife and I will have available each year, how much will potentially be left over when we die, and what kind of tax bill our children will be facing. That clarified a lot of things for us. Especially as, before working with Eric, we had never thought about what would happen to our wealth when we died and what it would mean for our kids.

Eric's note: Most people worry about whether they'll have enough money to see them through retirement. Wouldn't you rather have to worry about what to do with all the money that will be left over from your investments?

(Of course, that raises another problem: you also need to plan how to take care of the tax burden that wealth will put on your heirs when you die. This is the focus of the Succession Phase which you will read about later in the book.)

When it comes to the kind of lifestyle we're looking forward to when we retire, we don't want to compromise on things just so we can put more money away than we would ever need. We have a few major projects in mind, including selling our house and buying either a four-season cottage by a lake or a three-season cottage and a condo in downtown Montreal where we can spend the winters and enjoy some shows. We also want to travel, and we've already taken a few trips all over the world.

We've also been thinking about how we want to spend our time once we're not working. We both enjoy gardening, so wherever we end up living, I'll make sure there's some garden space. Also, we both like biking, so we have bought a tandem bike, and we will go out on it together as much as possible. Finally, we're both looking forward to many lovely evenings out with friends and family.

Whether everything works out that way or not, we'll see. But I'm comfortable that our finances are already in place to support that lifestyle. And the plan we built with Eric gives us more money for the first 15 years, so we can really enjoy those first years, and then once we start to slow down, we won't need to draw as much for the next ten years or the final stretch after that.

When I first met my old financial advisor, he spent half an hour telling me about the market: how it was moving, what was going on with gold and other products, international situations and how they could affect pensions and investment growth, etc. It was interesting, but it didn't tell me much about how to manage my portfolio.

My first conversation with Eric was very different. He didn't talk in broad terms about markets and the world economy. Instead, we discussed specific investment strategies that IT360 Financial was recommending in the current environment. We talked about my situation and plans, and the decisions I should make to implement those plans. He helped me understand how money moves, the impact of disbursements, and the importance of moving money strategically into the right investments to minimize my tax liability.

So, if you're reading this, I encourage you to think about the conversations you have with your advisors. Are they talking about the market in general terms, or are they showing that they understand your story? Are they talking to you about what will happen when you retire and, later, when you die? About how much money will be left? Have they run simulations about what that's going to look like? If the answer is no, you may not be talking to the right person for you.

Chapter 7

The Good Times

A few more years have passed. You either resisted the temptation to go back to permanent employment or went out, got the experience or promotion you needed, and now you've come back to contracting at a higher rate. You have multiple clients, so you're no longer dependent on just one contract, and you can finally feel confident that this will work out for you. Welcome to "the good times"!

Remember, however, that your finances are a highly complex machine: every component is connected to every other directly or indirectly. So, changing something in one part of the machine—tweaking a dial, changing the size of a cog wheel, adding an extra belt, or whatever—affects all the other parts.

The best advisors don't just look at their part of the machine. They understand how the whole thing works and what will happen if you change any of the individual components. It's about understanding the whole, thinking ahead, and understanding consequences (both intended and unintended).

If what you've read so far makes sense, but it's all new to you, you must ask yourself why you haven't been told about it before. The tools and strategies I'm describing are not new. Some of them have been around for over 30 years. However, as I said at the start of this book, financial advisors who are used to working with consumers simply won't think of them because they're irrelevant to 90% of their clients.

"Thanks, Eric, But I've got It All Handled."

Not everyone is lucky enough to find IT360 Financial at the start of their career as an Independent Consultant. Sometimes, they discover us after they've been in business for a few years. Then the big challenge is that they're used to the Broken Paradigms their old advisors have been following.

In these situations, we have to help the client see beyond those old paradigms, which can be painful. After all, they've been on autopilot for years, surrounded by well-meaning friends and family giving them half-remembered advice they read on a financial blog, and they're probably still talking to their old advisors.

Worse still, they don't always feel pain. They look at their accounts each month and see a strong portfolio and cash in the bank, and every year, their nest egg is growing. What they don't know, of course—and they have no way of knowing without the right tool—is what that fund *could* have been worth. They have no way of knowing whether the performance of their funds is great or merely good.

Maybe you're reading this, and your house is paid for or almost paid for, you have an investment portfolio that's growing, and you're on track for a comfortable retirement. But what if you could be doing even better? What if we could take things to the next level?

I see the same gaps in people's finances all the time: you know what you have, but how do you know what you don't have? So, if I could show you the gaps in your financial preparations, would you entertain some suggestions? Because whatever stage you're at and whatever your age, it's never too late to make adjustments. Financial health is like physical health. It's better to start exercising and taking care of yourself at 20. But if you're already 52 and your waistline is expanding, it's better to start at 52 than wait until you're 60! Even if you're 60, it's better to start now than wait until you're 70. You won't have the body you'd have had if you'd spent the last 40 years exercising, but you will be in better shape than the person who never starts at all.

Whether you're 30 or 60, and whether you've just started your business or you've been running it for 15 years, it's all the same to us. Your finances probably aren't optimized, and our job is to find the tweaks and adjustments needed to optimize them. Age is not an issue for any of these strategies. Even if you're over 60, many of them can be applied to your children (or even grandchildren)—remember, we're optimizing the finances of your entire family unit, not just you as an individual. And if you're at the other end of the age spectrum, we have sophisticated strategies to bring your parents into the equation (as long as they're still alive, of course!). The key to all of this is a technical term called 'insurability interest': a policy owner can claim an insurability interest in someone else (a need to insure them) as long as that person is either a key employee, a partner in the business, a parent, a spouse, a child, or a grandchild.

Everything starts with a conversation. Within 20 minutes, we have a pretty good idea of where the skeletons are buried by asking the right questions about the corporation, your personal finances, and the investments you already have in place (personally and through the corporation).

Critically, we don't expect you to scrap everything and start again from scratch. We create a plan that takes into account everything good you already have in place, but we tweak and adjust. It might only be two or three changes, but the effect of those changes will compound over time.

Book your own financial reality check and start planning your financial future. Whether you have existing advisors or you need support, schedule a discovery call with my team, and we'll make sure you're getting advice that's optimized for you as a business owner and independent professional.

https://consultant.financesti360.com/#book-a-meeting

Case Study 4

The Late Career Switcher: Maurice Chenier

Maurice Chenier is a great example of someone who has built a successful business as an Independent Consultant late in his working life. After a career that took him to some of the most senior roles in government IT, Maurice saw an opportunity to set out on his own and took it. And he is excellent proof that it's never too late to become a consultant.

I worked in IT in public service for 40 years, holding positions such as CEO of the IT Services Branch, senior VP, and Assistant Deputy Minister. During that time, I managed many large-scale domestic and international projects ranging from Free Trade Agreement automation with many countries to bringing our Canadian airports into the 21st century with things like the electronic passport kiosks that streamline arrivals processing.

When I retired in 2019, I considered just playing golf all day, but that didn't appeal to me. And I realized there's a real IT labour shortage in Canada and a lack of high-level experience, which will be critical as we try to rebuild the economy after the last few years. So, I decided that I couldn't stop working.

Instead, I set up a corporation and started working with large systems integrators in the US and Canada. I've been fortunate that the phone hasn't stopped ringing, and I've never had to go out and find clients myself. There's a huge demand out there for skilled IT executives.

It also brought home to me how fortunate I've been in developing the skills and experience I got from years of working in different IT and engineering environments. And I couldn't have wished for a better 'landing' after retirement: I love my work, my clients are happy, and the money is good. So, for now, I don't have any plans to stop (although my wife may have other plans for me!).

Paradoxically, when the Pandemic happened in 2020, I got even busier. The federal public health agency hired me to help manage many of the urgent digital requirements COVID created, like vaccine acquisition and distribution, vaccination records, contact tracing, etc. It's something I'm very proud of, although it's been intense.

As an independent professional, I can choose the scale and scope of my projects, decide how much risk I am willing to take on, and even whether or not I want to work with a client. Even better, I no longer manage thousands of staff across the country. Instead, I can focus on the project and its outcomes without juggling responsibilities for human resources, finance, procurement, and private sector contracts. And I'm more productive as a result.

Contracting has given me better money and more time with my grandchildren, and much of my work has been done remotely, especially in the last couple of years. Of course, if you try hard enough, you can always find downsides to everything. For example, as an Independent Consultant, you are highly paid. However, that means clients have equally high expectations in terms of output and contribution, which puts a lot of pressure on you, and it's easy to work very long hours—especially if you get caught up in what you're doing. So, you must take care of yourself and manage the client's expectations.

There's also the added complication that you're now a business owner as well as an IT professional. When I first incorporated, that was a concern for me because, even though I know IT well and have a master's degree in International Finance and Management, when it came to managing the company's money, I realized it wasn't my area of expertise.

Fortunately, a good friend connected me to Eric. All it took was one meeting, and I was convinced—and I'm generally hard to convince, especially when I'm paying good money for something: I expect a very high return in exchange. I'd already tried a few other options for managing my finances, and none worked out as well as this has.

One mistake I made when I started my career as an Independent Consultant was that I didn't incorporate soon enough. I started as an autonomous worker, which gave me the lifestyle benefits of being independent but none of the financial flexibility and advantages I would have enjoyed if I had formed a corporation. For example, I didn't have the protection that goes with being a corporation, the range of investments available to me was restricted, and I had much less flexibility in planning my taxes. Fortunately, Eric quickly got me on the right track, which was immediately valuable.

A mistake many people make is watching their portfolio in real-time, from day to day and month to month. As soon as something drops in value, they get scared and stop investing. But markets are volatile, especially right now, and investments fall and rise. So Eric taught me to focus on a 25-year window instead, which has made life a lot less stressful—and having everything managed by Eric and his team has also taken away much of the stress of running my own business as a consultant.

I'm not planning on retiring anytime soon—as far as I'm concerned, if you can continue to contribute to society, it's almost your duty to keep going. And I'm not alone in seeing retirement differently: more and more people are choosing to delay their exit from the workforce. Thanks to technology, you can still enjoy all the things people traditionally associate with being retired—staying home, spending time with your spouse and family, travelling the world, and enjoying as many healthy years as possible—while maintaining an active professional life. It's not necessarily about the money (although, for some people, it is). It's about other needs: the need to serve and be useful, to continue having an impact on the world, and to leave a legacy.

Thankfully, I'm at the stage in my career where I can be more open and have conversations with clients about my value that a younger person would hesitate over.

I hate being left out of the loop and underutilized. So, if a client wants to pay big bucks to get me, that's fine: when they hire me, I make it very clear that they're paying for an extra brain, not just another pair of hands at the keyboard.

Don't get me wrong. I'm a naturally curious person, and I love to roll up my sleeves and get involved. But the moment I feel a client isn't making the best use of my strengths and skills, I'll tell them they don't need to be spending money on me.

I know my strengths and my limits. When it comes to finance, I know I can't match the breadth of knowledge and experience that Eric and the IT360 Financial team have. And it's all under one roof, so I don't have to deal with four different firms to manage my money. Before I met Eric, I had a financial planner, an accountant, an insurance broker, and an investment advisor. Each of them took a fee, and I had to sort out what to do with all their advice. With IT360, it's a turnkey solution, and they take care of everything for me.

The Withdrawal Phase

Chapter 8

The Standard Paradigm is Broken (Again!)

The Withdrawal phase is about what happens when you retire. The aim is to take money out without

1. Compromising on your lifestyle
2. Running out of cash
3. Paying more tax than you have to (or leaving a massive liability for your heirs!)

As we've seen, most professionals advise their clients based on flawed, out-of-date paradigms that can be very expensive. The problem is, we've all heard the same tired old advice for so long that anything that doesn't fit the model seems wrong.

For example, if I told you at age 65 to put more money into growth stocks, you'd say I was crazy. As discussed in Chapter 2, the standard paradigm is to reduce risk and switch to less aggressive investment strategies by moving your money into fixed-income investments as you approach retirement. Then, when you retire, most advisors switch out of portfolio management mode altogether. As far as they're concerned, the portfolio is built, and it's time to take the money out.

Switching your money into fixed-income investments was great advice when 10% was a typical return. Today, however, returns are much lower, and if your growth is less than inflation, you're losing money every day. So, more than ever, you have to manage your portfolio just as actively in Withdrawal as in Accumulation. Unfortunately, while the world has changed, advice hasn't. So, it's a Broken Paradigm.

Sequence of Returns Risk

Throughout retirement, the value of your funds will go up and down because of changes in the market. The risk is that if you need to take money out while the market is down, any withdrawals you make will eat into your total funds more than they should, which can be especially dangerous in the early years of your retirement.

As a result, if you don't manage things carefully, you can deplete your pot much faster than planned—a phenomenon known as Sequence of Returns Risk. It's a bit of a hot button in the finance industry right now. Here's a simple illustration of what can happen. Imagine you've been investing with a goal of having $2 million in your pot when you retire, and you need $100,000 each year to maintain the lifestyle you want (note that these figures are just a fictitious example).

Now imagine the gods of finance are on your side, and just as you reach retirement, a market boom pushes all your investments up in value by 15%. Your $2 million portfolio is now worth $2.3 million. Even after you take out the $100,000 for your first year, you still have $2.2 million of assets to fund the rest of your retirement. Happy days!

But what if the market goes *down* by 15% instead? Now your fund is only worth $1.7 million on the day you retire, and if you take out $100,000 for the first year, that will only leave $1.6 million in the pot. You're just one year into retirement, but 20% of your fund is already gone. How will you live?

Broken Paradigm #6: Freezing Funds for Retirement

The problem is, of course, you can't control what happens to the market, and assuming you want a pleasant lifestyle in retirement, you're always going to have to take something out of your accounts. It's a nightmare for advisors, so most of them try to eliminate the risk in advance. That's why, as the client gets close to retirement, they'll move all their money into "safer" investments that, theoretically at least, are less likely to go down in value (but, of course, won't go up either).

The problem is that if your advisor is working with this broken paradigm, they'll probably advise you to start reducing risk two to three years ahead of retirement based on their projections of what the market is likely to do in that time. When you retire, however, you probably have 20 to 25 years ahead of you, not the two- or three-year window your advisor is using. The average time between market lows and highs is roughly 24 to 36 months. So, if you put all your funds into low-volatility investments now, you may cushion yourself from the impact of the next market dip, but over the next 20 years, you'll also miss out on half a dozen market highs—that's an expensive "cushion"!

So, what do you do instead? What you need is a holistic approach that considers every nuance of how your funds are invested and how market cycles work. Since cycles last an average of three years, it makes sense to transfer only the cash you need to see you through the next three years into safe-harbour investments. That way, you know that money won't be affected by what happens in the market. The rest of your funds stay invested with the same risk profile you were able to handle before retirement, and you manage the portfolio actively to minimize tax and maximize revenue.

> My dad is 77 and has been retired for a while. He always has three years' cash in the bank, and invests the rest just like he did when he was 50. Why? Because if I put it all into a low-risk portfolio, as the standard paradigm dictates, he'd have missed out on many opportunities to make money.

The Bucket Approach

We call this the Bucket Approach. It's a concept that is unique to IT360 Financial, and it refers to how we structure how you take money out of your company and when.

Here's how it works. Imagine you have the following financial assets, personally and in your corporation:

- Your company bank account
- An E-PP
- A TFSA

For each year of retirement, The Tool will tell us how much money you will need to meet your aims (not just your living expenses, but anything else you've told us you want to do when you retire, whether it's the holiday of a lifetime, a cottage, a boat, or whatever) and the best way to take money from each of those assets to minimize taxation ("You need to take 10% out of this account, 30% out of this account, etc."). But of course, there's a problem: that pesky Sequence of Returns Risk. What if you want to take money out for that cottage in two years, and something happens in the market in the meantime that destroys the value of your financial assets?

The answer is that, while the market is high, we withdraw enough money from the accounts following the recipe The Tool recommended to meet the next three years' needs (enough to see you through from one market peak to the next), and we put that in low-volatility investments. This is what we call "the Bucket," and as far as possible, we only take money out of that and leave the rest invested for the future. That way, whatever happens in the market, we won't need to touch the main accounts until the next market peak.

Throughout retirement, keep three years' cash in low-risk investments to see you through the current market cycle. Leave the rest invested smartly to take advantage of market highs while taking active steps to minimize the tax impact of your choices.

The mistake many people make is to freeze everything into cash or near-cash asset classes on retirement. They'll tell you the aim is to protect your nest egg and take out all market risk. But it is potentially an enormous waste and unnecessary if you apply the Bucket Approach. As long as you keep your bucket filled with cash that won't be affected by the market, you don't have to worry about market fluctuations because you will have enough money on hand to ride out the current economic cycle. This is what shelters you from the Sequence of Returns Risk, and of course, it's already accounted for in The Tool.

The point is not to eliminate risk but to balance it across your portfolio. That way, you're not taking on additional risk but also not missing opportunities to keep growing your pot.

So, even when you're retired, we still manage your portfolio to minimize tax and maximize revenue. And that means updating the plan every couple of years in line with changes in taxation and regulations and considering new opportunities.

Just because you've retired doesn't mean you can stop actively managing your finances—that's a recipe for running out of cash unexpectedly if the market shifts or the rules change. So, even once you start withdrawing, we're still in portfolio management mode, looking for ways to minimize tax (and other charges and claw-backs) and maximize gains.

Optimizing Retirement

Although preparing for retirement should inform your financial decisions throughout your career, once you get to within three to five years of when you want to stop working, it's time to start planning more aggressively. An easy mistake to make when you start taking money out to fund retirement is to look at your funds and those of your spouse separately. Throughout your life—not just in retirement but also in the Accumulation phase—you need to think about your family's finances holistically.

Here again, when we're helping our clients prepare for what will probably be one of the most significant changes in their life, The Tool comes into its own. Remember, we've used it throughout the Accumulation phase to plan where to invest. But The Tool isn't just about wealth accumulation. It's designed to allow us to see the implications of any financial decision, which means it also allows us to model the impact of decisions about withdrawal.

That's the beauty of The Tool. It's not an investment planning tool or a withdrawal planning tool. It's a financial tool: "one tool to rule them all." So, when it's time to live off your investments, we tell you which accounts to take money from to minimize taxation and maximize gain. In fact, the difference between an optimal withdrawal strategy and a traditional one can be as much as 20% in some cases.

The interesting thing is that a standard planning tool—the kind your bank manager will pull up on their computer when you sit with them—might tell you that you have just enough money to make it through the rest of your life, as long as you don't "overstay your welcome." We'll take the same numbers, put them into The Tool, and with some minor adjustments, maybe we can say, "If you make these changes today, you'll have more than enough." But it's not about reducing how much you take out—the aim is always to maintain or improve the standard of living. It's about changing how and when you're taking the money out.

> A potential client came to us just three years from retirement. He had his retirement plan through his bank and told us he was very happy with what he had. Even so, when I plugged his numbers into The Tool and made a few tweaks, I found him almost $500,000 more in liquid assets to enjoy in retirement!

Whatever age you are, it's never too late to tweak your pension arrangements

We've created a short online self-assessment that will model the long-term impact on your net worth of contributing to an E-PP vs an RRSP, along with answering other critical questions about how you manage your finances.

To get your detailed financial report and recommendations, visit:

https://consultant.financesti360.com/#compare-rrsp-vs-epp

Case Study 5

Work Because You Can, Not Because You Have To: Pierre Nelson

Pierre Nelson is a great example of an employee who looked at the consultants he was working with and thought, "I'm just as smart as they are. I should get paid the same."

I've been an independent IT consultant since 1995, working with government departments, non-profits, and private companies in Ottawa. Back in 1994, I was in my first full-time IT job. The hours were long, and the pay wasn't particularly good, but many of the people I was working with were consultants, and naturally, we got chatting. I soon realized that, as a salaried employee, there was a lot that I was missing out on. So, not long after that, I quit and went independent, even though I'd only been in the industry for three years.

Right from the start, I loved the consulting lifestyle. As an independent, I made almost double my old salary, but that wasn't the only benefit. It's easy for a permanent employee to get caught up in office politics. But as a consultant, I was above all of that.

There are also differences in how employers treat staffers and consultants—and it's not always in your favour! For one thing, they expect you to be able to do everything. The good side of that is that you get a lot of experience you might not have gotten as an employee. It's allowed me to grow a lot professionally and acquire skills and knowledge without having to go through formal training.

The biggest downside, of course, is that you don't get benefits—at least not from your client. As an Independent Consultant, it's up to you to arrange medical insurance for you and your family, prepare for retirement, make sure you're covered if something unexpected happens, and all the rest. And if you take time off, there's no paid vacation.

That leads into the other downside: unplanned time off between contracts. When I started, I was confident in my skillset, so I was never worried about security. Whether or not I got work was based purely on my skills and the value I created for my clients. However, my wives—I've been through a few!—were more apprehensive. They weren't comfortable with the idea that a contract could end and I'd need to find another one. But the reality is that even as an employee, you can find yourself in the same position: a company can lay you off, and there's no guarantee you'll walk into another job quickly. And it can take longer to go through the interview and hiring process for a permanent role than negotiating a consulting contract.

Fortunately, there have only been two times in all the years I've been contracting where I was "between contracts"—both times for about two months. In part, that's down to the breadth and depth of experience I have; I've always found it easy to get a contract. But also, in recent years, I've arranged things so that I'm working on multiple contracts simultaneously. That way, if a project ends or gets cancelled early, I still have money from other clients.

That's something employees typically can't do, especially in IT. Often, there are clauses in their employment contract that stop them from taking on second jobs. As a consultant, clients know they can't place that sort of restriction on me: legally, they'd be setting up an employer-employee relationship, which isn't in either of our interests.

Some people struggle as independents and go back. Speaking for myself, the only thing that would tempt me back into being a permanent employee is if there were something about a position that was very meaningful to me. I don't feel much need for affiliation; I'm happy being an outsider. A much bigger priority for me is taking care of my family. I have seven kids, five of whom are adults, so I'm making sure they're secure, settled, and have a home.

I'm one of those people who will try their hand at everything, so I don't rely much on advisors and experts. When I started as an independent, I set up the company and did all the accounting myself. Even when my income grew to the point where I was going to cross the threshold for the small business tax credit, I was confident I knew how to tackle it. But I booked an hour with an accountant to check that I was on the right track.

I got introduced to IT360 Financial through one of the HR companies I use to find contracts. Initially, I pushed back. I had previously reached out to a financial advisor. But, like most people in that profession, he was tied to a company and could only sell me that firm's products. If all I wanted was a set of investment products, I'm smart enough to research and find them myself. What I was looking for was honest, independent advice from someone who could recommend the best products in the market, not just the best products available from whatever company they were an agent for.

However, the person who told me about IT360 Financial really believed in what they do and assured me that they were building a plan, not just pushing products, and they would optimize that plan for me as the owner of a corporation. That intrigued me because it was an area that I wasn't familiar with.

I resent paying someone to do things I could do myself, but when it's outside my area of expertise, I want to work with someone who knows what they're doing. When I started talking to IT360 Financial, it wasn't the usual conversation along the lines of "I want to get you into mutual funds" (because you haven't got any, and it's on my checklist). The first thing they did was draw up a plan that focused not just on how to grow my wealth tax-efficiently but also making sure that I was prepared for the future—both the predictable (like retirement) and the unpredictable (like illness or disability).

IT360 Financial are also the first people I've spoken to who explained finances from both sides of the fence. They're looking at it not only from an investment growth perspective but also from the point of view of minimizing my tax bill. On the personal side, I understand finance very well—I'm what advisors call a "sophisticated" investor. But it was a real eye-opener to discover that I didn't have to take the money out of the corporation to invest it; that there are investment vehicles that aren't available to salaried individuals. A great example is critical illness insurance. If I get critically ill, I'll get a payout to help me through that period. But if I don't, then I get the money back in a tax-efficient manner.

Cash flow has always been a concern for me. I watch my cash flow six months out. But I also know that I will need money and somewhere to live as I get older. With seven kids—including four years when I was a single parent raising five of them alone—I couldn't always prioritize preparing for retirement. I needed to make sure the bills were paid, and my family's needs were met. Also, as a consultant, I don't pay into the Canada Pension Plan, so I know I won't receive anything from that in the future.

I'd already seen my parents struggle when they retired, before they received Old Age Security, and I didn't want to find myself in the same position. Luckily, I don't have to worry about that thanks to the plan IT360 Financial has created.

I was looking to diversify my portfolio, so IT360 Financial was the perfect complement to what I had been doing. The strategies IT360 Financial put together—incorporating insurance as an investment, a corporate investment portfolio, and an Executive Pension Plan—all made perfect sense together, and it's straightforward for me to see what position I'm going to be in when I retire, based on how much I'm putting in.

So, my old worries about struggling after retirement are gone, and I feel very comfortable about the future. And they've even been able to incorporate investments that I'd made in the past, like property.

Of course, retirement is still a few years away, but my intention is that once all my children have grown up and left home (the youngest is ten, so there's a way to go!), I will slow down. I'll probably still do some consulting because I like the freedom it gives me: I can pick a country, employer, and job that appeal to me, and I can spend six months on that contract, experiencing the culture and the food. Then when the contract ends, I'll come back, spend some time with the family, and then do it again in a different place.

At some point, that won't be possible anymore, but in the meantime, I'll push myself physically and mentally so I can stay healthy for as long as possible to enjoy life. The big thing is I'll be working because I can and not because, like most people, I have to. I'll work because I enjoy challenges and pick ones that align with my principles and values. Maybe I'll work for a charity because it's not about the money. One cause close to my heart is making sure people in developing countries have access to clean water. So, that could be something I choose to do. It's much more fulfilling than putting a cheque in the mail to a charity once a year and thinking, "I've done my part."

At IT360 Financial, I work with Sam Cellini, and something I really appreciate is that he doesn't just give me an answer when I ask a question; he gives me an *informed* answer based on actual experience and knowledge. A big problem in this industry is that there are many advisors out there who will give you advice that would be good *if* you were a salaried employee but not for a consultant running a corporation. You have many opportunities available that some advisors may not even know about, or if they do, they don't really understand them because they don't use them all the time.

So, you need to talk to people who do have that knowledge and understanding and, more importantly, have a plan for taking advantage of every path open to you.

The Succession Phase

Chapter 9

The Only Two Certainties in Life Are Death and Taxes

The Succession Phase focuses on how you transfer wealth tax efficiently to others—usually the next generation of your family. Most people don't realize how much tax there is when you die. If you only start to think about it when you're 70, it's probably already too late—many of the best strategies for optimizing your tax position are not even available to you in the later years of your life. So, it pays to start planning early; the earlier, the better.

There's a common misconception that Canada has no Estate or Inheritance Tax. While that is technically true—there is no federal tax officially designated as Inheritance Tax—that is far from meaning that there are no taxes when you die. Each province has its own way of getting money from you (or, rather, your heirs), but in broad terms, everything you own is deemed to be sold on the day you die, so it's subject to Income Tax and (apart from your primary residence) Capital Gains Tax.

Another common misconception is that you can transfer an RRSP to your children tax-free. Again, that is false: you can transfer it tax-free to a surviving spouse, but not your children. There is some relief for couples in that no tax is collected when the first spouse dies, but when the second spouse dies, CRA will come calling.

This brings us to the third (and possibly most dangerous) misconception about death taxes: who pays the bill? Many people assume that it will fall to their heirs. "I've got four kids," the thinking goes. "So, by the time everything is split between them, and they use their allowances and tax brackets, surely the tax won't be that bad?"

Broken Paradigm #7: Leaving Estate Tax Planning to Your Heirs

The problem is that tax on your estate is assessed on you posthumously, not on your heirs: if you leave a $1 million portfolio, CRA will tax it as though you had sold all the assets yourself, and your heirs will get their share of the *net* value. So, it doesn't matter what tax bracket they're in or what allowances they have. And to make things worse, it all happens on a single day. The transfers can't be spread over different tax years, so the tax bill hits you in one very large lump sum—as a result, as much as 25% of the money usually ends up going to the Government.

Now, whether you work with us or not, you will probably spend most of your working life trying to minimize how much tax you pay. So, it makes sense that as you think about the end, you can't stand the thought that the taxman will take it all back. And the sad fact is, this is a chapter most financial planners won't even talk to you about because their focus is often on what to do about your money while you're alive. As a result, most advisors leave Succession Planning until it is much too late.

At IT360 Financial, however, we plan and optimize well in advance. The aim is not to wait until you hit the wall: we know the wall is coming, so we plan for it 20 or 30 years in advance. That way, we can act on it today when there are many more possibilities open to you.

Let someone else pay!

There are two ways to pay taxes when you die. One, of course, is to pay them out of your estate using your own money. The other is to set aside funds to pay the final tax bill in your Estate Retirement Plan (which we used in the Accumulation Phase) and let your insurer pay the taxes.

You'll remember that at the start of the book, I mentioned that one of the main pillars of the Corporate Investment Policy is the clever use of insurance products that most advisors ignore, including the Estate Retirement Plan (ERP), which is designed to optimize your financial position both in the Withdrawal Phase and also Succession.

Without an ERP, you'd have to make decisions in your 40s about what to do when you're in your 60s or 70s. That's hard for most people to predict, so we use the ERP to make those decisions unnecessary. But you need to set it up early (so it's in place throughout the Accumulation Phase), not wait until you're almost at retirement age.

The point is that the tools you use in the Accumulation Phase should prepare you for succession planning. If you get that right, you don't need to do anything special—that's why we set things up the way we have, building estate planning into The Tool in every phase.

So, when should you start planning your succession? That's the topic of the next chapter.

Chapter 10

The Best Time to Start Planning Your Succession is Now

Estate planning is often dressed up with the fancy phrase "intergenerational wealth transfer," which makes it sound like something Bill Gates should be worrying about, not Joe Smith. So, another mistake many consultants make is that they assume estate planning and worrying about what will happen to your money when you die is only really relevant if you're very wealthy. And that's if they're not also putting it off because it's "something you don't have to worry about until you're old."

The sad truth is most people in their 40s and 50s aren't even thinking about estate planning; they're far more worried about whether they'll have enough money to see them through retirement. And because that's their main concern, it seems pointless thinking about what will happen to what's left when you die.

It's a natural fear, and most planners will tell you to play it safe and put more into the pot on the grounds that the more you put in, the more you'll have. So, people tend to focus on asset gathering rather than what they'll do with those assets later.

At IT360 Financial, we focus on asset gathering, too. But we also know that if we do our job well, there will be a lot left over at "the end." In fact, the chances are you'll have more than you ever thought you would. So, as we gather those assets, we're also thinking about where to put them to minimize taxation both during the Withdrawal phase and when you die.

You see, running out of money isn't the problem. Even if you're just well-off (rather than ultra-rich), you probably won't spend everything before you die. But you don't know how much you'll have left, which is why it's hard to think about estate planning.

So, as well as asking, "How will I make sure I have enough to see me through retirement?" you also need to ask, "Who's going to pay the bill on what's left over when I die?"

Think about it this way. In Accumulation, you build a portfolio of investments. In Withdrawal, you live off the income from those investments. Withdrawal is about transferring money from the corporation to you, but you don't know how many years you have left—it could be ten or thirty. So, as far as possible, you should be spending the income generated by your portfolio rather than selling the investments themselves, because you need that portfolio in place throughout retirement. If you start spending the capital, then at some point, there will be nothing left, which is what we're trying to avoid. In an ideal world, I want to show my clients a model and say, "Even if you die at 95, this is what will be left in each of your accounts."

So, if you manage withdrawal properly, those investments will still be there when you die. And we want to ensure those investments go to your family, not the taxman, so we want the intergenerational wealth transfer to happen as tax-efficiently as possible.

And here's something interesting to consider. The world is run by families that have figured out intergenerational wealth transfer. Each generation in those families is richer than the last, and the sooner a family figured it out, the more power and influence they wield today. So, there is no better time to start thinking about your family's intergenerational wealth transfer.

"Screw the kids! I had to work for my money. So should they."

It doesn't happen often, but sometimes when I talk about tax and inheritance, a client will tell me they don't want to spend time planning death taxes because their children should be grateful for whatever they get. After all, they didn't have to do anything to get it.

And that's perfectly fine. It's a choice. But I do like to point out that the client has been working hard with me to minimize the tax they pay. So, are they really telling me that, at the end, they want to let CRA take it all? That they don't care anymore? Usually, that's enough to change their mind.

As you've already learned, the strategies we'll be implementing aren't about compromising your lifestyle in retirement in order to leave more to your children. Instead, it's about organizing your affairs more efficiently so that the government gets less of your wealth, and it goes to your heirs instead—in effect, it's free money.

And the good thing is, even if you don't want to act on our suggestions now, it's never too late. If you change your mind later and decide you'd rather your family get your money than CRA, we can build succession planning into your financial plan at any point—even if you're already 65 (although, of course, as in most matters related to money, the sooner you implement these strategies, the better).

Doing good from beyond the grave

Of course, not all the money has to go to the next generation. Some of our clients want to leave at least part of their estate to charity. Many people assume that charitable giving is just for the mega-rich—that it's about leaving money to a hospital and having a tower named in your honour or giving it to a university and having a professorship in your name.

Charitable giving is about two things: doing good in the world and (of course) minimizing the tax on your estate. You may be dealing with fewer zeroes than Bill Gates or Warren Buffett, but there's still a tax liability, and CRA treats charitable donations very favourably.

> For the last ten years, I've been involved in an organization in Quebec that helps kids with addictions—drugs, alcohol, cyberaddiction, and others. I also took out a life insurance policy on my father. As a result, when he dies, that organization will receive a large sum of money. So, he gets to do good, even from the grave, and there's a tax break to make the deal even sweeter.

The way charitable donations are treated means that you could give to a worthy cause, and the actual cost would be minimal. If leaving $10,000 to a charity costs $10,000, you might donate or not. But how much would you leave if you could give a charity $10,000 and, because of tax breaks, the cost to your estate would only be $5,000 or even less?

There are strategies you can use to minimize taxation through charitable giving at every stage in life. Death is just one of those stages, with its own strategies. For example, you could set up a life insurance policy while alive, naming the charity as the beneficiary. Your contributions to that policy are tax deductible while you're alive, reducing your annual tax bill. Alternatively, you could leave the donation as part of your will, and a different set of tax breaks would apply. It's all a matter of understanding how tax works and having a playbook of strategies to minimize that taxation at each stage of your life.

"But, Eric, I don't have any kids!"

If you don't have children and you're not planning on having them, you might assume this chapter is irrelevant to you. But here again, the question is, who would you rather leave your money to: the taxman, a good cause you support, or perhaps someone else you nominate?

If you don't plan, the Government will plan for you. This way, however, you get to decide what you want done with your money, and we'll help you do more with it than simply paying taxes.

If you don't plan what will happen to your money after you die, the Government will plan for you!

Optimize As You Go

One of the big differences between our approach to estate planning and the standard paradigm is timing. Most people wait to think about succession until late in their life. Instead, you need to build it into everything you do throughout the Accumulation and Withdrawal phases. That way, succession planning and wealth transfer are already tax optimized when the time comes.

That philosophy underpins our whole way of working, from the conversations we have with clients and the plans we create, to how we built and use The Tool. That philosophy is there, guiding what we do, from the day we first meet you to the day we help your heirs deal with your estate.

And now that we've reached the end of the road, before we wrap up, let's look at how one of our clients has been building her legacy.

If you want to make sure your family will be taken care of, schedule a meeting with one of our professional advisors to review your existing arrangements, model your finances now and into the future and answer other critical questions about how you manage your wealth.

To set up an initial meeting, visit this web page and tell us how to get in touch. We'll take it from there.

https://consultant.financesti360.com/#book-a-meeting

Case Study 6

Doing Good by Doing Well: Ghislaine Boundjia

Ghislaine Boundjia has taken full advantage of the mobility and freedom that being an Independent Consultant offers and built a career on her own terms that allows her to make a positive impact in the world outside of the IT sphere.

I started my career as an engineer before moving into product management in my early twenties. More recently, I have moved into project management for telecom companies and financial institutions.

I set up my corporation and became an Independent Consultant in 2015. I wanted the freedom to take a career break if I decided (without needing to have a baby!). I also saw it as a way to achieve financial independence more quickly because of the enhanced possibilities it offered for savings and financial growth compared to being an employee.

At first, things didn't work out as well as I'd hoped. I set up my company on my own, and I made some critical mistakes in how things were structured financially. I also found it hard to get projects in the first few years because clients didn't think I had enough experience. They saw me as a product manager, not a project manager, even though I had a degree in project management and years of experience working in project teams! They would tell me that, while they believed I could do the job, I'd never had a formal position as a project manager on paper, so it was hard to justify my rates. So, when an opportunity arose in Africa to build a new career and personal path for myself, I took it. I started as a Technical Director, then moved into project management roles.

Making sure you have the proper certifications is critical in this industry. There are many options, but some are more recognized and highly valued by clients than others. For example, in Africa, I had a choice between doing the PMP (Project Management Professional) or the CAPM (Certified Associate in Project Management). Both are from the Project Management Institute and require roughly the same effort. But while both are recognized internationally, the PMP is better known and more respected. So, if I was going to put time into getting a certificate, I might as well get the one that would give me the most leverage in the market and earn me the highest rates.

For the same reason, once I got my PMP, the obvious question was, "What next?" Again, I didn't want to just pick a certification at random; I wanted to know what the market was looking for, which turned out to be ITIL (Information Technology Infrastructure Library)—an international certification that focuses on aligning IT services with the needs of the business.

Eric's note: A significant advantage of being a consultant rather than an employee is that you get to choose what you study and when. As an employee, your professional development opportunities are determined by the company, which is naturally more concerned with its internal needs than your career and marketability. As a consultant, you are free to look around and make decisions based on the opportunities you see, what skills are in the highest demand, and what will make you the most money.

When I came back to Canada in 2019, a lot had changed. The market was a lot busier for IT professionals, and the knowledge and experience I'd gained in Africa—combined with my PMP and ITIL certifications and the soft skills and self-confidence I'd developed (which you can't learn in school!)—made me a lot more marketable. Now, instead of chasing potential clients, they were coming to me.

One thing that not many people talk about in this industry is the challenges you face as a woman in IT (and even more as a black woman). Part of what led me to contracting was that I knew certain paths would not be available to me as an employee in a large corporation. If I stayed, I would have to give up on some of my dreams. So, while I missed out on the career progression and promotions I would have gotten inside a corporate hierarchy, I have won in other ways.

Being an Independent Consultant is not just about turning up, doing the job, and hoping the client likes you. And it's not only about the money and freedom—the lifestyle and financial benefits of being a consultant are great, but it's not fulfilling to me unless I'm also serving. From a personal perspective, it's very important to me to feel that I'm providing value to my clients. They are paying for my services, and in exchange: they get my services, experience, and capabilities.

The interesting thing is that Independent Consultants will often go above and beyond what's expected and what they're being paid for. And it's purely because of that desire to be of service and to create value. Unlike an employee, a consultant doesn't push themselves in the hope of getting a promotion or a pay rise. Their fee has been agreed, and they're just looking for more ways to provide value to the client.

Apart from having to give up any dreams of climbing the corporate ladder to the C-suite, I haven't so far found any disadvantages to being a consultant—although I realize I'm still relatively new to this career path. From a personal standpoint, it has been a very positive experience so far. Even if the market collapsed tomorrow, I still believe it has been the right move for me because of the financial growth and liberty, the freedom it's given me in planning and preparing for my retirement, and the mental and personal benefits. I feel more balanced and fulfilled, and I have clients who are grateful for the work I do.

One thing I did sooner than many professionals was to start thinking about my legacy. In 2002, just after I finished my engineering degree, I set up a non-profit foundation to provide education scholarships for children in Africa. My heart has always beaten for Africa, and it is a cause that is very close to my heart. So, with my studies over, I wanted to do something useful with my time.

I have always felt fortunate that I had parents who could pay for my studies, and I wanted to give other children the same opportunity. So, I started to raise money. At first, it was maybe 1,000 Euros a year. But now we've been going for over 20 years, and the amount has grown. Some years have been good, others not so good, but from a personal standpoint, it didn't make a difference: all that mattered to me was that there were children who knew that there was a woman in Canada who cared about them. And my business has provided me with the freedom to give more.

Retirement is still a long way off for me, but in any case, like many Independent Consultants, the idea of retirement is relatively meaningless (even more so for me because Africans don't have that concept—in many African languages, there isn't even a word for retirement!). So, it's more about looking forward to slowing down and getting pickier about how much stress I will tolerate, which clients I work with and how much time I want for myself.

I see myself in those later stages of my career probably in similar roles to now but creating more value. Or perhaps I'll move into portfolio management. Whatever move I make, I will make sure there is a market for that kind of work as a consultant. For example, I love product development, but that's traditionally an in-house role. So, if I moved into product development today, it would probably mean becoming an employee. Therefore, I'm most likely to stay in project and program management, where there are many opportunities for consultants. But I'll look for roles that give me the flexibility to travel more so I can work more closely with the children I sponsor.

Eric's Note: For many Independent Consultants, finances are almost an afterthought. They plan their career in detail, thinking about what qualifications to get, what kind of experience they need on their resume, and the sorts of companies they want to work for. But they see money as an output: "I'll get my clients, do the work, and see how much money I can make as a result." It often takes a conversation with a financial specialist for them to see that you can be much more intentional and structured in how you approach your finances. However, Ghislaine had a bit of a head start.

I come from a culture that is very focused on family and people, and I grew up with a very intentional mindset around money. As a consultant, I firmly believe it is critical to manage your earnings. I was lucky that I'd been brought up to take care of finances. However much money I have, it's vital to me to live below my means so I can save for the future.

Another part of planning for the future is having the right insurance policies in place. But, unless you're in that world, it's hard to keep up with all the available products and to know how to structure things so you don't end up paying more tax than you should. Working with Eric and his team has helped me fine-tune my approach. I'm not a finance expert, and I rely a lot on common sense to make my decisions, but with Eric, I have the right inputs for those decisions.

Chapter 11

Conclusion

Regular financial planning is—let's face it—boring. When you talk to a new financial advisor, they always ask the same questions: What will happen if you die prematurely? What if you get sick? What if you live too long? These are essential questions that you need to consider and plan for, but as you have seen in this book, there is another way to look at financial planning, and for most people, it's a much more exciting way to meet traditional financial planning objectives.

If you've reached this point in the book, one thing should be clear: standard financial advice paradigms do not work for you. It's not that the advice is wrong or that the advisors who give it are incompetent. It's just that the industry is set up primarily to serve employees: T4 employees make up 90% of the working population, so it's natural that most advisors should focus on them and that most products should be designed to meet their needs. However, you're not like 90% of the population. You're a business owner, which allows you to play according to a completely different set of rules—but you need an advisor who knows those rules and who understands when, where, and how to apply them.

Everything we do at IT360 Financial is designed around two simple goals:

- To minimize the amount of tax you have to pay
- To maximize the gains you make.

The key to that is to understand how everything fits together. The financial system is complex, and a slight change in one area of your finances can have a significant impact—for better or worse—in other areas. If you don't have that understanding, something you do today might save you thousands of dollars in tax or set you up with a very large and unwelcome bill. Similarly, well-intentioned attempts to minimize risk now could cost you many dollars in lost future revenue and potentially wipe out what little returns you might make.

It's hard for a single advisor to have the necessary depth and breadth of knowledge of every aspect of the financial environment, which is why it's in your interest to work with a multidisciplinary team of experts who are used to thinking beyond the narrow confines of their specialist discipline. Finding those experts takes time, and it's hard to recognize whether you've found the right people. I know because I've assembled that team already in IT360 Financial. Which is why I have an invitation for you.

If what you've read in this book makes sense or at least makes you curious, I would love you to jump on a call with me or one of my team. We'll explore your current finances and the arrangements you have in place, make suggestions, and at the end, you are free to choose whether you want to continue to work with us or prefer to try to do things on your own.

Let Me Be Your Partner

Our whole approach at IT360 Financial is built on the idea of partnership. I'm not here to sell you anything. Instead, I'm here to educate you and show you a different way of doing things. Unlike many advisors, our approach is not "I'm the expert. Trust me, shut up, and listen while I tell you what's good for you." Rather, my goal is that you'll end up knowing just as much as me. For example, if I present you with three options, I will also make sure you understand precisely why option B is better than A or C, even if you're not financially savvy, and that you know the impact each choice will have on your wealth today and in the future.

When we meet with a potential client, we don't just ask a few questions from a checklist. We ask a lot of questions, and we explain even more. We suggest and propose, and you make the decisions. But you can only do that if you understand the decision you're being asked to make. Of course, once you've made a fully informed choice, we'll implement the exact strategies you want us to implement.

It's never too late to begin taking care of your finances, and the sooner you get started, the less you'll lose out on.

Whether you're starting out and want to ensure you're optimizing your financial affairs so you don't pay more taxes than you need to; more established and want to make sure you're making proper provisions for your retirement; or nearing retirement, and want to make sure you can fund the lifestyle you've been aiming for, schedule an initial meeting by visiting this web page. We'll take it from there.

https://consultant.financesti360.com/#book-a-meeting

www.ingramcontent.com/pod-product-compliance
Lightning Source LLC
Jackson TN
JSHW080730180125
77230JS00002B/39

* 9 7 8 1 9 8 8 1 7 9 7 0 4 *